SEXUAL BEHAVIOUR
IN ANCIENT PERU

PLATE I

Coitus. The woman, in a supine position her head
turned and the man's chin resting on it. This piece
today is an extraordinary expression, so beautiful
and exotic that its authenticity could be doubted.
North Coast (Pativilca? XIII Century?). Light
wood, partially painted in red and white; height
9.5 cm. Albert Fehling Museum (Lima).

C O V E R "Carcancha" with penis erect. The animated-corpse or "carcancha", covered only with a cloak, is playing an antara, or pipes of Pañ, a musical instrument which with notable frequency is related to the world of the "carcanchas". Moche. Privat collection.

Printed in Lima - Peru, by Grafica Morsom S. A.

Sexual Behaviour

In Ancient Peru

Federico Kauffmann Doig

Professor of Peruvian Archaeology and History of Ancient Peru, at the Federico Villarreal National University, Lima. Director of the Art Museum, Lima (1960-64 and 1969-71). Director of Conservation of Cultural and Monumental Patrimony of Peru (1979) and Vice-Director of the National Institute of Culture, Lima (1971-72).

KOMPAKTOS, S.C.R.L.

LIMA - PERU

Preface. 5

INTRODUCTORY CONSIDERATIONS

SEXUALITY EXPRESSED IN ARCHAEOLOGICAL TESTIMONIES

S U M M A R Y

PREFACE

This book is the result of repeated examinations of pottery with sexual themes, and of field observations carried out by the author, especially in the region of Lake Titicaca, where he considers that a sort of "phallic cult" can be traced in mushroom-shaped stones and in funerary towers (chullpas), which, like the ones of Sillustani, up to 12 meters in height, seem to reproduce phallic contours exposing the gland (KD, 1976: 271-72). The direct examination of archaeological pieces was supplemented by reading the chronicles and modern works about sexuality in pre-hispanic Peru, among which the pioneer study of Rafael Larco Hoyle (1966) and Paul Gebhard's examination (1970) based on statistics must be especially mentioned.

The author became interested in this subject in 1957, when he worked at the National Museum of Anthropology and Archaeology (Lima), and kept the key to a small room where the collection of pottery on sexual themes was jealously kept and could only be visited by specialists or people bearing special credentials. The situation is different today: since 1959, for example, the new Art Museum in Lima, under the direction of the author, has placed on display to the general public all the pieces in its collection related to sexuality... At that time the author wrote a brief note on the subject (KD, 1963: 149), amplified in another work (1966: 28-32) published when the edition of the fundamental book of Larco was announced (1966). In both his notes, based on statistical estimates and personal observations, he decided to attack the tangle of unfounded reports which circulated in whispers concerning the "depraved habits" of the Incas and especially of the protagonists of the Moche culture.

During the sixties and seventies he extended his information and he prepared a study for presentation at the FIRST ANDEAN ARCHAEOLOGY SYMPOSIUM, held in Warsaw in July 1975; a symposium which he attended as an official guest of the Government of the Socialist Republic of Poland thanks to the organizer of the event, the Peruvian Ambassador R. M. Pereyra. The work was entitled "Sex and Mythology", which was also the original title of the present study and which comprises three sections. Of those, only the first, intended to trace sexuality in ancient Peru through archaeological material, is now going to print. The two remaining sections, which refer to sex in the Inca Empire in the light of the information given by the chroniclers of the XVI and

5

XVII Centuries, and of the myths related to the subject —also obtained from this type of source— will form, respectively, the second and third volumes of this work, which for publishing reasons will be edited separately.

The pottery pieces forming the basis of the study compiled in this first section come, mostly, from the National Museum of Anthropology and Archaeological (Lima), in which institution the author worked for some years; from the Art Museum, also in Lima; from the Albert Fehling Museum (Lima), repository of rare pieces; and from the Rafael Larco Herrera Museum (Lima), which possesses perhaps the most important collection of archaeological material concerning the sexual behaviour of ancient Peruvians.

Fig. 1. Deities copulating. Representation in which sexuality appears elevated to the mythical sphere of procreation (Relief in a Pativilca container, based on the Tiahuanaco-Huari cultural tradition. National Museum of Anthropology and Archaeology, Lima - Carrión, 1959).

ACKNOWLEDGEMENTS
For facilities of study given to the author: National Museum of Anthropology, Lima. (L. G. Lumbreras, H. Rosas L., E. Versteylen). Art Museum, Lima. (Sara de Lavalle, F. Untiveros). Alberto Fehling Museum, Lima. (A. Fehling). Brüning Museum, Lambayeque. (O. Fernández de Córdova). Rafael Larco Herrera Museum, Lima. (Rafael Larco Hoyle). Mr. and Mrs. Figuerola, Chepén. For assistance in photographic takes: Messrs. F. Allert and E. Casallo, Lima. For drawing the sketches: Mr. Evaristo Chumpitaz, Lima. For suggestions after reading the first edition of this work: Dr. M. A. Denegri, Lima. For translation from the original Spanish text: Mrs. Mariana Mujica de Salazar, Lima. For supervising the English translation: Miss Mary Nickson.

INTRODUCTORY CONSIDERATIONS

1. *Historical Background*

The archaeological process in Peru covers three cultural eras or periods. The most ancient of these eras, which starts more than 20 thousand years ago, is characterized and determined by a "parasitic" way of obtaining food (collection: hunting, fishing, vegetable harvesting), and the typical places corresponding to this are Pacaicasa, Lauricocha, Toquepala and "pre-ceramic" Ancon; the following era starts around 7 thousand years ago and is dominated by a primitive economy, a sort of incipient farming mixed with traditional hunting. One of the places which typify this era or period is Huaca Prieta, discovered by J. Bird in 1946. Only the third period characterizes the wide base of ancient "Peruvian culture", also classified as "Central Andes"; here, sustance is derived mainly from farming, which, in the last instance, is what causes Peru to be considered as a "high culture" (1). The Central Andes comprise geographically what corres-

(1) The type of sustenance explains the cultural "level"; farming generated, in ancient times, a complex culture. Before agricultural production man lived closer to the animal world, precisely due to the "primitive" ways in which he obtained his aliment. Fishing played an important but not dominant role as a food during the apogee of the "high culture" on the Coast...

ponds to modern Peru, and the Andean Region, of which it is part, to the territory occupied by the Tahuantinsuyo, or Inca Empire, which extended through South America, covering the Pacific coast between parallel 3, north latitude, and parallel 36, south latitude.

The Peruvian "high culture" starts about 3 or 4 thousand years ago and extendes to the Inca Empire, which reaches its eclipse with the Spanish conquest during the first third of the XVI Century. It is in the "high culture" age that direct information regarding sexuality can be detected, expressed through representations of pottery, textiles, etc. Such information is not given in uniform intensity or style; it keeps step with certain variations in time and geography. In any case, it is necessary to underline that the "high culture" stage appears in Peru with common denominators derived substantially from a similar economic activity: the one mentioned of intensive land cultivation. However, we are not in a position to discern all the reasons that caused one particular culture to be more expressive about sex than others, in the general consensus formed by the different representations of the Peruvian high cultural stage.

It is the changes reflected especially in pottery that have led to a division of the archaeological process into periods corresponding to the high cultural age. Its course begins in an eloquent way with the so-called "Chavín"; this first period of "high culture" is also known as "Formative", because in it are present the cultural bases on which further cultural development rests, until the arrival of the Spaniards in Peru. (KD, 1978: 86-92).

In the scheme that divides the "high culture" of Peru into Cultural Horizons, the Formative period is the oldest of the three: the Early Horizon. The concept of Horizon has been discussed and defined by W.C. Bennett, G.R. Willey and and J.H. Rowe, among others.

To explain it in a simplified way, the three Horizons (Early, Middle and Late) are three periods in which the presence of artistic-cultural traits, more or less common, can be respectively noticed. These traits are particular in that they appear dispersed over a wide geographical area, covering the major part of the Central Andes (Peru, Bolivia) and even the whole Andean Region in the case of the Late or Inca Horizon. The cultures known as "Chavín" (Early Horizon), Tiahuanaco-Huari (Middle Horizon) and Inca (Late Horizon) are considered characteristic of the three Horizons or cultural expressions of a broad geographical base. The factors which impelled the propagation of these cultures of "panperuvian" aspect were probably religious (Chavín) mixed with imperialist forms or power search (Tiahuanaco-Huari, and Inca). The Horizons are separated by periods called Intermediates. Between the Early and Middle Horizons, we have the "Early Intermediate" period, and between the Middle and Late Horizons, the "Late Intermediate" period.

The important thing about the Early Horizon is not that it shows different religious-artistic expressions united more or less closely by style. It is based, mainly, on the fact that during this period the presence of all the typical cultural elements, common to the high culture of Peru, which will continue to be present with slight stylistic changes until the arrival of the Europeans, are already insinuated: votive pottery, monumental architecture, corn and other cultivated plants, etc.

The Early Horizon opens around the IV Century A.D., with a period of an apogee in craftmanship: the Early Intermediate, with cultures of defined regional features, such as Moche (Mochica), Nasca, Recuay... Regional governments become strong and social classes are marked, belligerence is common. In addition to human sacrifices (which mark the previous period: Chavín, Sechín...) there is now a definitely combative spirit, with rivalries, seeking to dominate neighboring groups (1). Around the IX Century A.D. "hegemony" is attained by the Tiahuanaco-Huari culture, by means of creating an empire with central and coercive powers; in other words, the Middle Horizon. After a few centuries, with periods of apogee and internal problems, the Tiahuanaco-Huari Empire loses power,

---

(1) All that is stated above is evidenced by the Sechín and Chavín iconography, with a richness of images; just as in Mochica iconography, in the Early Intermediate Period (KD, 1968: 163, etc.).

8

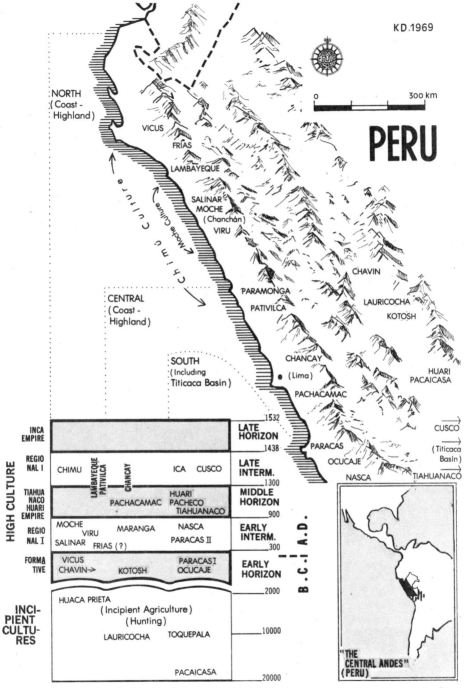

KD.1969

PERU

NORTH
(Coast - Highland)

VICUS
FRÍAS
LAMBAYEQUE
SALINAR
MOCHE
(Chanchán)
VIRU

CHAVIN
LAURICOCHA
KOTOSH

PARAMONGA
PATIVILCA

CENTRAL
(Coast - Highland)

SOUTH
(Including Titicaca Basin)

CHANCAY
(Lima)
PACHACAMAC

HUARI
PACAICASA

Chimú Culture
Moche Culture

0   300 km

1532
1438
1300
900
300
2000
10000
20000

PARACAS
OCUCAJE

CUSCO
(Titicaca Basin)
TIAHUANACO

NASCA

HIGH CULTURE								
INCA EMPIRE						LATE HORIZON	1532	
							1438	
REGIO NAL I	CHIMU	LAMBAYEQUE PATIVILCA	CHANCAY		ICA	CUSCO	LATE INTERM.	
							1300	
TIAHUA NACO HUARI EMPIRE			PACHACAMAC	HUARI PACHECO TIAHUANACO			MIDDLE HORIZON	
							900	
REGIO NAL I	MOCHE VIRU SALINAR		MARANGA FRIAS (?)		NASCA PARACAS II		EARLY INTERM.	300
FORMA TIVE	VICUS CHAVIN→		KOTOSH		PARACAS I OCUCAJE		EARLY HORIZON	2000
INCI- PIENT CULTU- RES	HUACA PRIETA (Incipient Agriculture) (Hunting) LAURICOCHA TOQUEPALA PACAICASA							10000 20000

B. C. I A. D.

"THE CENTRAL ANDES" (PERU)

9

allowing a renewing of the regional cultures developed before Tiahuanaco-Huari. This occurs around the XIII Century A.D. and corresponds to the Late Intermediate Period.

The Chimú, Colla, Chanca and Inca cultures are typical of the Late Intermediate Period; the latter, still circumscribed by Cusco and its neighborhood. Each struggles to impose its hegemony. This is achieved by the Inca group from Cusco in the days of the Emperor Pachacútec. After defeating their inveterate enemies, the Chanca group, in 1438, Pachacútec and his son Tupac Yupanqui swiftly dominate the Colla and Chimú and many other —less powerful— ethnic groups who inhabited the Andean Region. In this way the Tahuantinsuyo or Inca Empire (Late Horizon), is formed. This enormous Empire which extended longitudinally in an unbroken line over thousands of kilometers, begins to collapse before it reaches a century from its founding. This takes place in the XVI Century, with the arrival of the Spaniards; symbolically, in 1532, with the execution of Atahuallpa, the last of the Incas or Emperors of Cusco.

2. *Research Sources*

Just as all the archaeological culture of Peru is mainly detected through two principal sources, and through others of secondary importance, from the information they supply, the sexual life —which is a part of and linked to a larger cultural context— is also comprehended by means of those two prime sources. Archaeological material originating in that remote past constitutes one of them; the other major source corresponds to the written word, introduced by the Spaniards, which recorded, in the XVI and XVII Centuries, fragments relating to sexual habits and to sexual mythology. In both cases the theme of sex was considered within a greater context, as has been said; even more, its importance was minimised in the chronicles as well as in the majority of archaeological representations. That is to say, as will be seen in more detail in the following pages sexuality suffered the impact both of inhibitions and taboos when dealt with by chroniclers, priestly or not in the chronicles written in the XVI and XVII Centuries, and by native artists of the most diverse Peruvian cultures prior to the conqueror Pizarro, save for rare exceptions. This is the case of the Moche ceramists; and even the Moche ceramists limited it in their exposition because, as shown by the author on the basis of estimative percentages (KD, 1966: 30), the sexual ceramic pieces produced by them form an insignificant portion compared to the amount of ceramic representations bequeathed to posterity which cover the most diverse expressions of their cultural sphere...

The archaeological material related to sexual themes is comprised mainly by sculptural or aesthetic pottery coming from the Vicús and especially from the Moche culture. Moreover, Moche produced an important amount of pottery painted in a schematic but realistic way, with figures and scenes in dark red over cream or white, re-

10

lated basically to supernatural and mythical sexual concepts. While sculptural pottery is rich in profane (or almost profane), as well as supernatural scenes, paintings with sexual meaning are somewhat scarce and limited to the magic-religious sphere. It is interesting to note that in pre-Moche times, sexual representations are practically absent, and when they do appear, they can only be found associated to the world of images of high religious hierarchy. The hermaphrodite character of the most ancient gods, or even their asexual character, can be traced to the beginning of the high culture, more that 3 thousand years ago [Fig. 2].

Apart from the pottery representations mentioned there are very few sexual images made from other archaeological material. Something may be found in textiles; but, according to known testimonies, these are not sexual scenes represented in textiles, but groups illustrating human sacrifices in which prisoners or subjects chosen for sacrifice appear, with their genitals visible because they are shown naked... This kind of scene has its counterpart in iconographic arrangements made of stone, as in Sechín; but in this culture —as in many others of ancient Peru— indications of sex are almost entirely absent. Archaeological material on the sexual theme, or delated to it, covers other expressions, such as the chullpas or funerary towers, in which the author sees the representation of giant phalluses, which will be dealt with separately. The guacanqui, or love amulets, made of stone, are only known through references made by the chroniclers.

Fig. 2. Inverse insistence towards the asexual, from the most ancient archaeological iconography; except for cases like this one in which the deity is given a penis and semen (Tello Obelisk, Chavín).

11

There are also sexual iconographic elements involved in the sphere of archaeological material, which appear, exceptionally, in other materials: metals, for example, as ancient as the ones of Frias, and as 'recent' as those of the Inca Empire; or in stone, from the Tiahuanaco-Huari period.

The other important source mentioned is the written one. It refers to all that the Spaniards collected from the past, prior to the Conquest, and to their observations about the habits and rules that governed sex in the days when they discovered and conquered the land of the Incas. In fact, the authors of the chronicles written in the XVI and XVII Centuries were not only Spaniards; there were also crossbreeds, like Garcilaso, and Indians like Guaman Poma, who gathered valuable information. We remember here all that has been said about sexual inhibitions, and how erroneous it is to see 'censures' with Occidental cosmovision, since in Peru we find them, from very ancient times; just as in the Old World there are, as is known, sexual taboos which are even pre-christian...

It is unnecessary, in a work like this, to review all the writings of the XVI and XVII Centuries, or even to present a historical criticism. This is because the sexual theme, linked as it is to a larger context, represented by the information of the chronicles in all their length, is subordinate to a general basic criticism or hermeneutics to which the ancient writings have been treated by various scholars, such as J. de la Riva

Agüero, R. Porras y C. Araníbar, in the Peruvian context. It only remains to state that the author does not agree that this source —that of the chronicles and all written documentation— should be despised. This is why we consider that R. Larco is unfair when he says that: "I have been able to carry out this self-imposed task in everything related to love expressions of the Mochicas and other peoples of pre-columbian Peru, resorting to the sole source of study material: the contents of the tombs" (Larco, 1966: 137). Not only can the presence of the written source of the XVI and XVII Centuries not be denied: even more, we have to admit the importance of this type of compilation; it is inadmissible to neglect consulting them. It is not only that their information is more abundant than is generally supposed. They are unique in various aspects: not particularly, it is true, for learning details of the "erotic" Moche, but to have an integral knowledge of sexuality in ancient Peru. And all this, naturally, admitting the limitations of these works and of their authors, with the taboos of the time; taboos from which, even in the XX Century, neither the common man, nor the erudite, have been able to free themselves. Seen thus the written source of the XVI and XVII Centuries holds on the subject that interests us a wealth of information to be selected and processed. It is this source that informs us —but never with the range and precision demanded by the scholar— about the constitution of the family, adultery and its severe punishments, dynastic incest, acllas or chosen women, pampahuarmi or whores, about religious homosexuality, about aphrodisiacs, institutionalized collective orgies and conception magic, about the myths that constitute the precious material of "oral literature" that come from remote ages, etc. And these subjects —and not only erotic pottery— are also included in the sexual sphere, so that they must be included in a study on sexuality (1).

To the written sources of the XVI and XVII Centuries, which should be understood to include the information contained in the archives (2), must be added the ethnographic source of the survival

of ancestral habits. Thus, the servinacuy, or first phase of marriage still exists, and also the chiaraje or competitive deeds of sexual vein, etc., on which we have, respectively, specialized works by Marzal (1977: 141-209) and Gorbak-Lischetti-Muñoz (1962).

3. *The Sexual Sphere*

The sphere of sex is not limited only to coitus, nor to voluptuous caressing. It covers a broad spectrum which is projected over a great part of cultural dynamics. That is why an analysis of the theme, apart from the examination of archaeological testimony, should include some sections about sexual habits when the Spaniards arrived in the Inca Empire, and about prehispanic mythology... Creation is a fact that borders on sex though apparently this aspect can be disregarded by elevating it to a mythical plane. It is in this wide sense that the author wants to develop this study on behaviour (and feelings) concerning sexual matters among ancient Peruvians. This book then apart from the first section dealing with what one might almost call profane love, eloquently expressed in archaeological material, will also comprehend basic subjects necessary for a general understanding of the theme: the family, cosmogonic and anthropo-

---

(1) On this occasion we will not stop to analyse and evaluate recent studies. Many of them will be mentioned in this work and are included in the Bibliography at the end of this book. But we have to mention, apart from the major works of Larco (1966) and of Gebhard (1970), the observations of Urteaga Ballón (1968), Terrazos Contreras (1973) who has gathered an interesting group of sexual pottery, the diverse thematic investigations of M. A. Denegri (1977, etc.) and the survey carried out by D. Treneman ("Gente", Lima, 30.3.1978). Years earlier, Posnansky (1925) devoted his notes to what he classifies as "horrifying sexual pottery", and Muelle (1932) published a brief study on the theme. Finally, from 1963 and 1966 come the notes of Kauffmann Doig already mentioned, written independently of the study by Larco (sp. edition: 1966) the most complete work regarding archaeological material of sexual content until Gebhard published (1970) his monograph. However, the analysis of sexual archaeological pottery pieces starts with Brüning (Muelle, 1932: 67) at the beginning of the present Century, though the monograph of Lafone Quevedo can be considered as a preview, based mostly on historical information.

---

(2) Thus, for example, in the "cases of witchcraft" of the Archiespiscopal Archives, in Lima, abound details of sexual context, as can be seen in the documents themselves and through publications of part of said Records: v. gr. the study by Basto (1957).

13

Fig. 3. Sexuality is not limited to copulation. This miniature figure represents a priest, or chaman, with a movable penis; one foot can also be moved. Note the feline character of one of the hands (Piece of laminated gold and silver repoussé and soldered. Filigree work marks some details. Frias. Weight: 28 gr. height 7.5 cm. Brüning Museum, Lambayeque).

gonic myths, fertility rites, etc. (2).

In other words, the mystery of procreation and fertility in nature are subjects that man, through comparison, links to his own sexuality and to his erotic emotion [Figs. 4, 5, 6]. He considers them as forms of creation, differing only on diverse planes... and man, under the shelter of magic, ends by wanting to be lord over the laws of nature. First we find him trusting that the drawing of appropriate or "propitiatory" figures will influence the multiplication of animals, which he hunted and needed for survival; the paintings of Altamira, and, in Peru, those of Toquepala, are famous examples of this. After several thousand years, man learnt the secrets of fertility in nature, he cultivated plants and raised animals for his sustenance. But here also he noticed his impotence in the face of calamities such as long droughts, and to exorcise them he continued using magic rites, ever more complicated, in order to bring those superior powers to submission: to have them work for his benefit... And that rite, directed precisely to fertility, explains a considerable part of archaeological representations of sexual content: phallic figures of diverse kinds, celestial coitus, etc. [Fig. 1]. The projection on human fertility embraces, undoubtedly, not only the sectors of representations already mentioned: it "shows" in inhibitions which lead to the genitals not being frankly portrayed... Very few and debatable are the figures that show sex and which dissociated from all mythical context come to be an expression of pure eroticism. That, of course, does not deny the presence in all ages, of the forces of libido, which are instinctive, and of resources secretly invented by man in all ages in order to intensify them.

(2) They form independent studies. A preview of these themes is offered in the Appendix of this work.

14

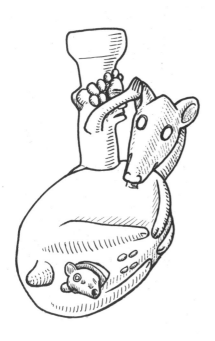

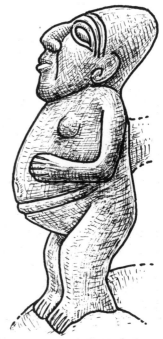

Fig. 4. Container showing the birth of a llama (Chimú, height 18 cm. Art Museum, Lima).

Fig. 5. Pregnant woman (Lambayeque, figure; height 11 cm. Art Museum).

Figs. 6, 6a: Container showing a birth scene. Two "midwives" are helping the expectant mother (Moche, National Museum of Anthropology and Archaeology, Lima).

6

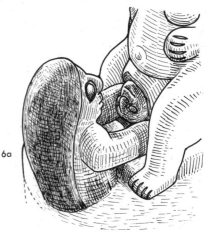

6a

SEXUALITY EXPRESSED IN
ARCHAEOLOGICAL TESTIMONIES

1. *Sex Taboos?*

Due to the fact that this work includes archaeoloical material concerning sexuality specifically, a superficial view of the book could lead to the assumption that, in ancient Peruvian cultures, every action was conditioned by or related to sex.

Without wishing to detract from the importance that the ancient Peruvian gave to the world of sexuality and eroticism, it is necessary to clarify that, on the contrary judging by the sculptured and painted ceramic figures of that time, it cannot be said that there was an insistence on producing objects of a sexual nature neither should it be said that there was an overflow of such representations, which from today's point of view might be considered as "pornographic".

Very much the contrary. Except for the isolated case of the Vicús and Moche, whose archaeological representations will be commented on in the next chapter, a general view of the iconography on sexual matters seems to indicate that in ancient Peru, little attention was given in art to the evocation of sexual scenes and perhaps none or on a very reduced scale to pure eroticism.

Furthermore, the author considers that the major part of archaeological representations with naked figures show them as asexual; and this is especially noticeable when the figures appear within a marked magic-religious context (KD, 1969).

If in general the expression of sexual themes is conspicuous by its absence, what could have led to that? Perhaps, an excess of "modesty" linked, in that case, to moral rules converted into rigid sexual taboos? What has been said about the poverty of sexual representations can be proved from the very start of the Peruvian high culture, some 3 or 4 thousand years ago, up to the Inca Late Period, about 500 years ago. The exceptions that can be found on this point seem only to prove the rule; everything that has been said can be corroborated by a general examination of the vast legacy from the archaeological Peru of all ages.

2. *Exceptions: Vicús and Moche*

The Moche culture was developed in the North Coast between the IV and IX Centuries A.D. It is related to phases of typical Vicús, which are estimated to be perhaps more than two thousand years old. These two cultures, and especially

Fig. 7. Taboos on the representation of sexual themes are found throughout all ancient Peruvian cultures, excepting those located on the North Coast (Vicús/Vicús vessel. D. Seminario former Collection).

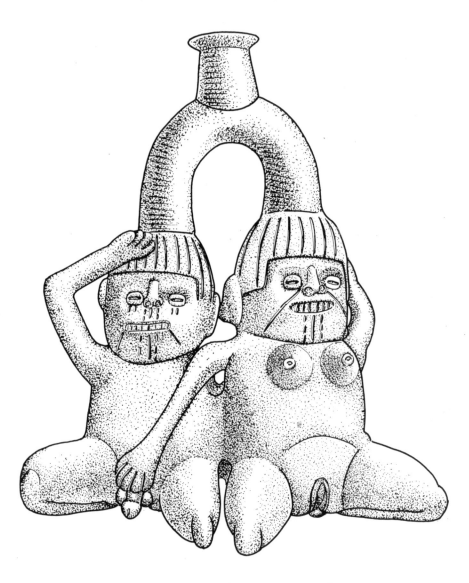

Fig. 8. Frank scene with apparently no votive overtone, of a woman caressing a penis. Both persons are naked and show their genital organs in a natural way (Salinar. Rafael Larco Herrera Museum, Lima).

the Moche, are the exception. In fact, most of the expressions regarding sexuality in ancient Peru were produced by the Vicús and Moche artists; sculpturally moulded in clay and transformed into objects which were functional containers and vessels.

The Moche people teach us not only about different positions assumed in coitus, but in "erotic subtleties", such as fellatio or oral coitus; they also "describe" sculpturally, anal coitus between man and woman and even show cases of homosexual relations. These representations caused the Moche culture (or Mochica) to be considered as "perverse", "degenerat-

Fig. 9. The Moche ceramists-sculptors are the only ones who represented sexual scenes in a natural way: The Vicús follow them. However, the series of representations on a sexual theme with no votive intent are scarce. Pottery with a sexual theme generally appears balanced, if considered within the whole context of Moche pottery (Fellatio scene, Moche III, Rafael Larco Herrera Museum, Lima).

ed", etc. (1). However, those who so branded it, did not take into account that the proportion of figures on the sexual theme is quite small (some one thousand in the National Museum of Anthropology and Archaeology), in relation to tens of thousands of Moche sculptured pottery which represents other phases of their life... Due to the fact that the Moche represented all their cultural world in pottery, it would rather have been symptomatic if they had omitted sexual themes (KD, 1966; 1969). The fact that in Museums and among collectors it is a common practice to group together and isolate this kind of representations brings them into prominence and makes them appear more numerous than they really are. Moreover, the fact that years ago museums did not show these "erotic" groups to the general public led to the popularisation of legends such as the one that said that "homosexuality was then quite prevalent"; when there is only one specimen showing this practice in an obvious way, though this naturally does not eliminate the probability that it was more extensive than iconographical testimonies would indicate.

Finally, as can be seen throughout this work the author considers that the entire sexual iconography of ancient Peru is in some way, to a greater or lesser extent, imbued with a votive content.

3. Nakedness without Eroticism

The representation of naked subjects, in which sex is naturally represented, refers to sculptural (Vicús and Moche) and painted pottery (Moche), depicting prisoners with a rope around their neck and arms [Fig. 10], and with their hands tied behind their backs; perhaps these in part were people destined for sacrifice (KD, 1976: 90). Textiles from the North Coast, considered as Chimú, also show scenes of this kind [Fig. 11],

Fig. 10. A warrior, captured and stripped of his clothes being pulled by a rope (Moche, Amano Museum, Lima).

---

(1) Posnansky (1925) thought, for example, he discovered a relation between the "horrifying" Moche pottery and practises of craneal deformation. Thus, he attributes those images to "extreme deformation (that) suffered by the region where the libid centers are situated..." and he concludes that perhaps the "brain abnormality", was the reason for a pathological state of "non-satisfaction" from the sexual point of view. (Posnansky, 1945-57 v. 2: 250-51, plate LXVIL, E, F, G, H.). Valdizán (cit. Muelle, 1932: 71) also speaks of a "pathological state", as an explanation that among the Moche not "one single way of abnormally performing the libido sexualis" was lacking; he sees there the cause of a "cocaine psychosis" which could have affected the "libido centers". It was Muelle (1932) who attacked the pathological theory applied to the Moche sexual pottery, and who also replied categorically to the adjective "pornographic"... Muelle emphazises that, above all, in the explanation of the Moche sexual pottery, the "cult of reproduction" must be considered though, as is natural, he could not entirely avoid the concepts held in the thirties, about sexuality which he shows when arguing that "one can make a great work (of art), even though the artist be perverse" (Muelle, 1932: 72).

Fig. 11. Scene of human sacrifice elevated to a mythological plane, where the personages appear naked. As in the preceding figure, here again no erotic overtones can be found, even though the genital organs are represented. The scene is similar to the stone figures of Sechín (KD, 1978: 197). Chimú. Cloth (A fragment, shown by H. Reichlen).

elevated to mythical planes (KD, 1978: 197). In any case here we are not faced with what is known as "exhibitionism", since no erotic intention is perceived in the figures. Not even in the "Frias Venus", a naked figure, is there a breath of eroticism [Fig. 12].

Other examples of nakedness without eroticism are provided by the small figures of men and women, of the Inca period, worked in silver and gold [Figs. 13, 14]. In a certain fashion, the examples mentioned should not even be considered as nudes, since they are small realistic human idols, certainly given a sex, but which were dressed [Fig. 15]; their connection with the fertility cult seems evident.

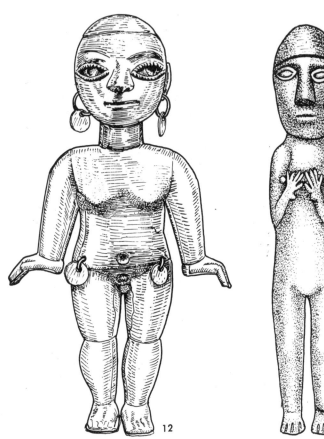

12   13   14

Fig. 12. Example of nakedness without eroticism, bordering on the sphere of the asexual.
A small hollow figure: a sort of "bottle", with
a head which can be turned and removed,
forming the stopper of the metal recipient.
(Frías — gold and platinum [eyes]; soldered
plates: height 15 cm.; weight 60 gr. Brüning
Museum).

Figs. 13-14. Two small figures, man and woman, with slightly pronounced sexual characters. Probably small idols of low hierarchical
magic-religious spheres (conopas?). Perhaps
these figures were dressed, as in the figure on
the following page (Inca cast metal).

Fig. 15. Small anthropomorphous figure, similar to those described on the preceding page,
with its nakedness covered by a robe, fastened
by a large pin or tupo (Inca; metal and cloth;
Ethnographic Museum, Berlin).

Fig. 16. Ceramic representation of a naked
woman; the pubic hair is prominently figured
and perhaps it corresponds to tattoos of sym-
bolic design (Nasca).

Fig. 17. The Nasca ceramists only exceptionally
represented sexual scenes. These are involved
in a magic background (Late Nasca; schematic
figures painted in red, ochre, black and white;
height 14.5 cm. Albert Fehling Museum, Lima).

15

16

17

Even in the group of Moche representations where people are shown indulging in sexual intercourse, one discovers as will be seen in a later chapter, that the man is almost always dressed in some or all of his clothes; even during coitus he does not remove his breech-clout. In bed, the couple is covered with a blanket, and if the artist leaves the genitals exposed, it is only to obtain visual effects.

In all that has been said about nakedness and "exhibitionism", the only exceptions are the Vicús and Moche vessels that show penises of enormous size [Figs. 7, 57]. But these representations had a specific magic-religious function, as will be seen later; they are not, therefore, an exaggerated exhibition of the genital organs of "satyrs", as has been affirmed, and as regards nakedness, it is appreciated that these figures are partially dressed. Some cases of "exhibitionism" also appear in Nasca iconography, but they are generally female and even here it is difficult to find examples which could be considered as nakedness with only an erotic function [Fig. 16]

4. Asexual Figures of Chancay and their Widespread Tradition

The subject of nakedness is closely related to the figures which are commonly called "cuchimilcos".

The "cuchimilcos" abound in Chancay culture, but are also present in other contemporary cultures (i.e.: Ica). But their tradition is very ancient and widely diffused: Las Aldas, Curayacu, Paracas, etc. [Figs. 19, 20, 21]. Further-

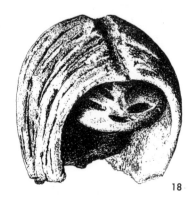

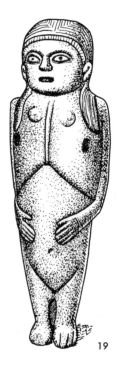

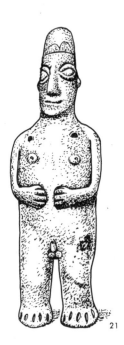

Fig. 18. Female head, fragment of a pottery-sculptural representation from Valdivia, Ecuador, where the tradition of the cuchimilcos appeared more than 4 thousand years ago (Publ. H.D. Disselhoff). Fig. 19. Hollow female ceramic figure, from Curayacu (Lima), some 3 thousand years old, in which the tendency towards an almost asexual representation of the human body can already be noticed (N.M.A.A., donated by F. Engel). Fig. 20. "Huari" pottery figure, another example of the tendency towards asexual iconography. Fig. 21. Alto Marañon pottery figure in which sexual characters —in this case, male— are shown but in minimized form. XIII Century A.D. (N.M.A.A., Lima).

24

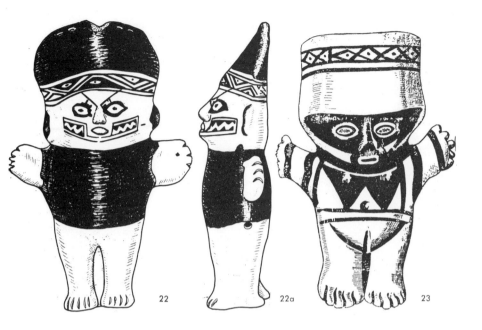

Figs. 22 y 22a. Chancay cuchimilco, asexual but probably female, front and side view (Art Museum, Lima). Fig. 23. Another Chancay cuchimilco in which the female sex is shown, but not insisted on; the breasts are scarcely hinted. The cuchimilco, simply because it appears naked or almost naked, must not be classified as a sexual representation (N.M.A.A.). Fig. 24. "Chinese" type Chancay vessel, in which the navel is represented and the extremities are shown but not the genital organs (Art Museum, Lima).

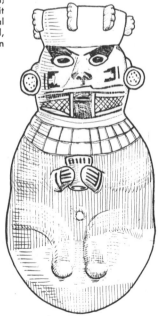

more, due to its great diffusion the cuchimilco becomes a Panamerican cultural model spread through all pre-hispanic American culture. An Andean version, perhaps the most ancient cuchimilco, is already present in the Valdivia Culture (Ecuador). It is more than 4 thousand years old.

The cuchimilco is a terra-cotta figure, of more of less human shape. At first sight, in the case of Chancay [Figs. 22, 23], it is difficult to identify its sex; but the cuchimilco is a female figure, even though neither the vulva nor the breasts are indicated or even clearly marked (1). These figures do not reveal any voluptuosity whatever; they are almost asexual and therefore very different from the small stone female statues of Willendorff and other sites in Europe, which apparently belong to the Paleolithic, age dating back more than 50 thousand years. In spite of the almost asexual charac-

---

(1) Exceptionally, there are male cuchimilcos, with their genitals depicted with neither exaggeration nor voluptuosness.

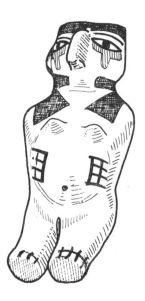

Fig. 25. Small compact terra-cotta figure, showing a woman, perhaps pregnant. She is rather fat, and reminds one of the "Willendorf" from the Old World (Nasca, height 16 cm. Art Museum, Lima).

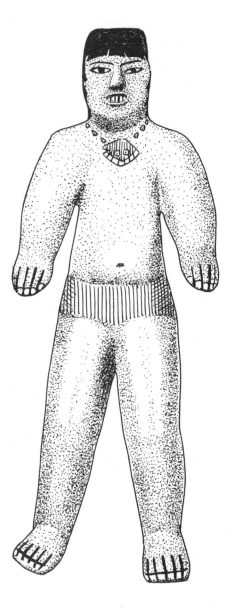

Fig. 26. Representation of a young woman. It does not have the votive character of the preceding figure, but perhaps it can offer a clue from which to reconstruct standards of archaeological beauty (Nasca, N.M.A.A., Lima).

teristics of the cuchimilco —a stereotyped figure, mainly in the Chancay version, which occupies our attention— it is probable that these figures may also have had their place in the magic-religious sphere, and for this reason must be set within the context of the fertility cult: sometimes symbolized by only a female body which perhaps personifies the pachamama or "mother earth" (KD, 1969; 1978: 597-9).

5. The "Peruvian Willendorf" and other Nasca Female Figures

The compact, burnt clay figures of the Nasca culture constitute a separate section among the representations of naked human figures. Here one finds a definite intention to show the human body emphasizing its sexual organs. The figures are generally seated women, naked, with facial and corporal tattoos and voluminous buttocks; the breasts, however, are not very pronounced [Figs. 25, 28].

There are exceptions, in which the figures do not show fleshy protuberances. These specimens would appear to portray young and sexually attractive women, dressed sometimes in a brief tunic: they seem to be models of the beauty of the times [Fig. 26]. There are no male versions corresponding to the little figures described. In these "Venus of Nasca", sexuality it would appear is exposed naturally, they show a certain though moderate degree of eroticism which can be "lived with" even by the contemporary observer...

Also from Nasca come the jars which picture naked women with tattoos or stylizations in the Mount of Venus, their legs halfspread; in these figures, a votive air can be seen, which is also noticed in the richly dressed figures of "ma-

Fig. 27. Grouped faces of a young woman, similar to that shown on one of the figures of this and the preceding page, but in this case they are painted. Note the locks of hair on both sides of the faces (Nasca. Tracing: Beatriz Neumann).

Fig. 28. Compact terra-cotta figure showing a young woman, front and side view. The breasts are not visible. She is naked, with corporal paintings or tattoos on legs and buttocks, which are quite prominent. It appears to be a representation connected to some concept regarding procreation. However, the "Chinese" eyes and the lock of hair on the side of the face seem to indicate that the ceramist might have wanted to portray, in this figure, an ideal type of beauty of those days (Late Nasca, height 16 cm. Art Museum, Lima)

trons". The case of the "Matrons of Nasca" seems to correspond, however, to representations of women of high social or religious rank, with no erotic content whatever (1).

6. Genitals represented separately

The presence of paintings and sculptural ceramic copies of sexual organs separate from the human body, female as well as male, deserves special mention. Save for rare exceptions (Nasca particularly), the few samples of genitals represented isolatedly belong to the Vicús and especially to the Moche Culture [Fig. 29].

Vessels with beaks converted

---

(1) From the Nasca culture also comes a limited quantity of coitus scenes among which the face-to-face seated position appears frequently.

into realistic and enormous phalluses, are relatively frequent in Vicús pottery; from them, one would be forced to drink... Male sexual organs depicted in Moche pottery show the testicles and the penis, with the prepuce folded back showing the gland. These were drunk from, thus converting, them into a sort of instrument of artificial fellatio. Likewise, these objects and the ones previously mentioned are not just representations of sexual organs; they have a function and, therefore, are grouped in a separate series which includes other types and are studied in Chapter 19.

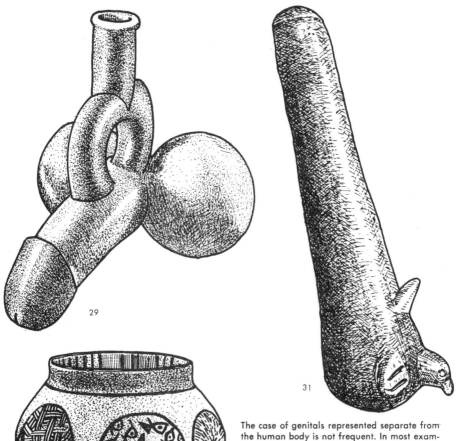

29

31

30

The case of genitals represented separate from the human body is not frequent. In most examples the representations are functional. Fig. 29. Such is the case of this phallus with an orifice from which to drink in a ritual act (Moche). Fig. 30. A series of vulva, with only a figurative intent, with slight votive significance (Nasca). Fig. 31. A ceramic whistle in which perhaps a phallus shape can be discerned (terra-cotta). A little bird is shown at the base (Private Collection).

32

33

Figs. 32-33. Two Moche sculptural pieces showing two subjects tenderly caressing each other. In the top figure the woman masturbates or caresses the penis.

In other cases, we find representations of only the vulva (Nasca), where the clitoris and large lips are portrayed with anatomical precision; there is here no other function than a simple portrayal with hardly any votive content [Fig. 30]. The Vicús tripod vessels, where the feet are transformed into phalluses, which will be seen in Chapter 21, also form a special case (Larco, 1966: fig. p. 129).

The phallus-shaped whistle of the Moche culture is rare and can be included in this section, in spite of the fact that it is not of itself a phallic representation. This is not the case of the containers representing camouflaged phalluses of human forms, which are examined separately; nor the vessels representing figures with genital organs from which to drink, and which will be mentioned later because they are not representations of isolated genitals. The stone phalluses of the Titicaca region are not mere copies of the male penis; their magic-religious function is evident and it leads us not to include them in the present group of isolatedly represented genitals.

In conclusion, the representations of genitals represented separately are mostly dependent on some function.

7. *Amorous caresses, kisses, and genital handling*

Except for those forms, generally slightly defined, of caressing, which can be explored in coitus scenes, in fellatio, in "masturbation" or in the handling of male genitals and in which corpses frequently take part —formulas which will be reviewed separately— there is a limited group of pottery that represents amorous caresses and heterosexual genital handling of an erotic, unductual, or perhaps precoital, essence.

A classic example is that of a Salinar jar, from the Rafael Larco Herrera Museum [Fig. 8]. It is one of the few examples known in this culture (1). It shows a sitting-kneeling couple in which the individuals, naked, are side by side, with the thighs in a half spread position; meanwhile the woman places her hand on the still flaccid penis, and both lovers have one hand to their heads, while the man seems to embrace the woman round her shoulders.

Gebhard (1973, 8: 25) finds a relatively large quantity of Moche jars (22%) representing genital caressing and handling, although it is true that he includes here the surrealist cases of caressing where living corpses take part, and which in this present work are examined as a separate group.

The lovers caress and handle each other, generally seated, intertwining their legs and embracing each other with one hand, while with the other the woman touches or masturbates the virile organ

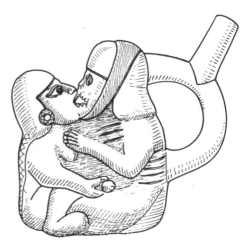

Fig. 34. Oral contact and caressing between a carcancha and a woman (N.M.A.A., Lima).

Fig. 35. A eunuch —judging by his prominent breasts (gynecomast) and lack of sex— caressing the vulva (Piece described by R. Larco. Rafael Larco Herrera Museum, Lima).

(1) Gebhard assures having recorded in general, only twelve Salinar pottery pieces, all anthropomorphous: four female figures; four male figures representing penial erections of prominent phalluses; two figuring the coitus (the woman lying and the man upon her, and kneeling in the other example), and finally two of heterosexual caressing (9: 22).

[Fig. 32]. The woman's chin is often caressed meanwhile by the man; exceptionally, the female breasts are touched, but cases where these are sucked or kissed are not known [Fig. 33].

The kiss is sometimes represented but very rarely; always in relation to corpses [Fig. 34]. The living corpse introduces its tongue into its female partner's mouth, or in other situations, the tongues of both touch each other. The participants in caressing acts are usually dressed; sometimes the woman is shown naked, while the man is dressed. It is not always possible to define the degree of nakedness, due to ambiguity in the representation.

It can be concluded, generally speaking, that love caresses are almost absent in pottery representations on a sexual theme, even during coitus; and that genital handling was practised by the woman, in order to stimulate the man's libido and prepare him for coitus, or perhaps only as an act of a masturbation...

8. *Positions in Coitus*

There were several variations of positions in coitus and on that subject Moche pottery is the most illustrative. However, there are earlier representations of Vicús, though somewhat sublimated and transported to mythological planes; they show mostly the position from behind or the ventral-dorsal position, in which the woman assumes a posture that resembles a quadruped [Fig. 70]. In other scenes

32

36

37

38

Different positions adopted in coitus. Some of them are variations. The examples correspond, approximately, to the nine positions described (Fig. 36, Chimú; Figs. 37-40, Moche; Fig. 41, Coastal Inca; Fig. 42, Moche; Fig. 43, Recuay; Fig. 44, Vicús/Vicús).

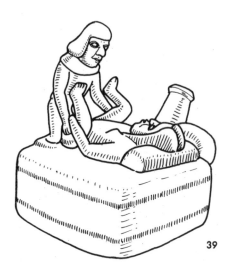

39

41

40

42

43

44

the woman offers herself standing, with her back turned and also supine [Fig. 44].

Intercourse between seated couples is found specially in the Recuay and Nasca cultures [Fig. 43]. The Chimú vessels continue, in a less eloquent, varied and artistic way, the tradition of their Moche predecessors regarding the position adopted during coitus. Apart from the cultures mentioned, representations of coitus are almost or entirely unknown.

When reviewing the Moche pottery with a sexual theme, P. H. Gebhard (1973, 9: 9-15) finds eight coital positions, but warns that these "are somewhat restricted: five explain virtually all of them..." And he adds that "other positions, mostly unclassified variations of the preceding positions", totalize only 4%. He finally points out that "there are no examples of coitus in which both participants are standing or sitting (the woman with her back towards the man), kneeling face to face, or curved round sideways. He specifies the positions mentioned below, to which can be added one more, present in the Vicús pottery, where the participants appear standing (Nº 9). Of these postures, all but one of which appear in Moche pottery, some (Nº 1) are found in the Salinar and Virú cultures; others, as Nº 8, are repeated in cultures contemporary to Moche (Nasca, Recuay), and in later cultures (Chimú).

1) The woman supine and the man above her (Moche: 9%).

2) The woman on her side as well as the man behind her like one spoon placed behind another (Moche: 29%).

3) The woman on her side, and the man on top of her, but only partially; or otherwise, in a crouching position, close to the woman's backside; in both cases, vaginal or anal penetration is from behind (Moche: 9%).

4) The woman lying supine, and the man kneeling or crouching between her legs (Moche: 9%).

5) The woman kneeling or on all fours and the man also crouching or standing behind her (Moche: 18%).

6) The woman prone (lying face downwards) and the man also prone, on her back, or behind her crouched between her buttocks (Moche: 18%).

7) The man supine with the woman on top of him, kneeling or sitting (Moche: 3%).

8) Both seated, face to face (Moche: 2%).

9) Addenda: Coitus between man and woman, both standing, the woman with her back to the man; penetration, anal or vaginal is from behind (Vicús) [Fig. 44].

Coitus takes place, in these "natural positions", frequently per anum, between man and woman. In addition oral or per os coitus was practised. Both practices and other "aberrations" will be reviewed separately —Chapters 10 and 11— and after a brief look at the context in which the sexual act takes place.

9. Background and Context regarding Coitus. Absence of stimulating gestures and Collective Scenes

Positions adopted in coitus are assumed within a particular context. Coitus does not take place on the pampa(*). It is done on a bed formed by a blanket or matting spread on the floor, and a pillow made of cloth rolled or at least tabular in shape; a blanket, sometimes decorated, covers the bodies [Fig. 47]. The ceramist leaves legs and sexual areas uncovered, as a means of "portaying the act central to the scene"... In some cases the woman seems to rest, lying on her belly, on a natural or artificial elevation of the ground. Generally, the woman but rarely the man, copulates naked: he is generally wearing a breech clout, which is loosened for the act, or he is represented as fully dressed.

Coitus scenes show the woman's complaisance, or at least a degree of passivity that permits the assertion that scenes of violence, rape, sadism or masochism were not intended to be represented. Larco (1966) and also Gebhard (1973, 9: 13) notice even a certain degree of lack of interest in the sexual activity on the part of the woman: "Some lie passive, only cooperating by adopting a certain position, others hold or wrap their legs around the man, some of them facilitate introduction, guiding the penis or displacing their buttocks" [Fig. 45]. Beyond that, nothing shows caressing, nor kisses appearing during coitus; in breast mani-

(*) *Pampa*... quechua word meaning plain, or open ground.

pulation, the man merely holds the woman's breasts.

But neither does the man appear particularly excited or panting [Figs. 47, 48]. Only in one case is there the suspicion that an attempt has been made to show male orgasm: though even here there is no expression of excitement with open mouth, facial contorsions or semi-closed eyes [Plate XII]. Larco was right in noting that this is not due to the incapacity of the artist-ceramist who, when he wanted to, admirably copied in clay different psychic expressions. In certain specimens, in which solitary masturbators or caressing couples are portrayed, the Moche artist has reproduced facial expressions reflecting these states of mind. On the contrary, during coitus, he insisted in showing an impassive man.

All couples having intercourse represent adults. There is only one unductual case, which seems to show paidophilia: an adult woman apparently masturbates a child, according to a figure shown in Chapter 12.

In coitus scenes only one couple is shown. At the most there is a third person: a sleeping or nursing child, resting on the belly and breasts of the mother, while the man and the woman lying on their sides copulate from behind [Fig. 48]. In these cases, we are shown by copulations where the couple appears in the family bed; perhaps too behind this kind of representation there is a symbolism, as mentioned in the next chapter. An extraordinary case is that of a man copulating, per anum, a young girl, while the latter sleeps between

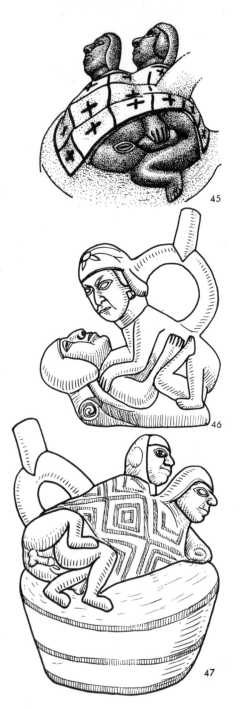

45

46

47

48

her parents, who also seem to be in a deep sleep [Fig. 49]. For their part, the examples given in Recuay pottery, where several women appear surrounding the scene of coitus, need not be interpreted necessarily, as cases of collective eroticism, of a man receiving erotic attention from several women simultaneously; it means that those women appear to be patiently waiting their turn, if they are not simple spectators, since in several examples they carry a libation vase in their hands [Fig. 50]. They are, probably, sexual representations elevated to a magic-religious plane, as seems to be demostrated by the Moche scenes in which the man adopts the figure of a deity (Chapter 16). But this does not mean that the author flatly denies the possibility that these could be representations of a high-ranking man surrounded by his women, as the existance of male polygamy or poliginy in those times is taken for granted.

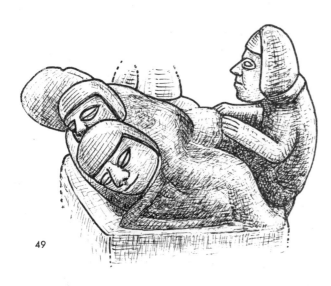

49

Fig. 45. Coitus taking place under a blanket, where the woman to introduce the penis helps by guiding it (R. Larco Herrera Museum). Fig. 46. Perhaps the man during orgasm (N.M.A.A.). Fig. 47. Most coitus representations are shown without facial expression. Fig. 48. Coitus per anum in the "family" bed, perhaps to avoid pregnancy. Fig. 49. A young woman between her parents, is copulated while she pretends to be asleep (Pub: V. W. v. Hagen).

Fig. 50. Mythological personage copulating, perhaps accompanied by his concubines (Recuay, N.M.A.A., Lima).

10. Sodomy, or Heterosexual Anal Coitus

It is surprising that in Moche pottery showing coitus scenes, the sexual act is done, very frequently —perhaps more frequently than is generally accepted, even by some specialists— through the so-called anal coitus, or "sodomy". Gebhard (1973, 9: 11-12) asserts that the percentage is minimal (21%) but admits that he has not taken doubtful cases into account. And he

adds that "in several other cases, body positions suggest anal coitus, but the genital organs are hidden, or not clearly modeled". In a general calculation, Larco (1966: 110) remarks that more than 95% of heterosexual relations with genital contact took place by "coitus per anum". KD (1966: 30), after examining the pieces at the National Museum of Archaeology, concluded that cases of cohabitation took place between man and woman, "but in most cases it was per os" (a word he wrongly used referring to anal coitus). On the contrary regarding anal coitus, some say that "from a detailed study of numerous vessels, in only a very few could its existence be affirmed" (Ravines, 1974: 12).

The practice here referred to must be separated, strictly speaking, from homosexuality, because though penetration by the male sex organ is per anum, it is not between individuals of the same sex. Even in the XVII Century this habit had extended to the north coast as can be seen from the confessionaries adapted for the natives of that region (Carrera, 1644). Ancient authors, like Cieza (1553) appear to lump together or confuse heterosexual and homosexual anal coitus in what they call "the infamous sin of sodomy".

It is the woman who accepts this variation of coitus. Perhaps it was she who introduced "sodomy" since this method of intercourse was contraceptive, as already noted by the author in 1964 (KD, 1966: 28-31 and Colophon), in a monograph published independently of Larco's study (1966). Some re-

A considerable percentage of coitus representations show cases of sodomy, or heterosexual anal coitus (Figs. 51-52); perhaps practised impartially in order to avoid pregnancy and as an erotic variation to stimulate the libido (Moche, N.M.A.A. and R. Larco Herrera Museum).

51

52

presentations, in which a child is shown in the conjugal bed, seem to suggest this [Fig. 52] Garcilaso (1609: I. IV c. XII) refers to the fact that while the child was breast-fed the parents "abstained from coitus, as they said it was bad for the milk and weakened the child...". This, however, does not exclude the possibility that heterosexual anal coitus could have been practised indistinctively: as a contraceptive, as well as an erotic variation to stimulate the libido. In that respect it is meaningful that the child does not always appear in anal coitus scenes [Fig. 51].

Finally, Larco (1966: 101) mentions the case where the deity Aiapaec is shown in an "anti-natura" act; that is, practising anal coitus.

11. Fellatio, or Oral Coitus

Oral coitus, or penis sucking, is apparently represented only in Moche, Lambayeque and Chimú potteries, which are, after all, the most expressive ones of Ancient Peru. There are no known representations showing this act between men. No cases of self-fellatio have been registered (1); nor are there scenes in which "animated corpses" take part (2). In the same way, there are no representations referring to male oral contact with the vulva, or cunnilingus (3). Oral genital contact was, therefore, done by the woman, judging from available representations; that is, fellatio was practised in a typical way [Figs. 53, 54, 55, 56].

In the act of fellatio the man appears naked, or halfnaked, and even occasionally fully dressed; the woman also may be dressed or not, as shown in the cases where it can be recognised, when the iconographic ambiguity is not emphazised (1). In most fellatio cases the man is seated; he also appears lying supine or resting on one side, and very seldom is shown standing. In fellatio if "the man is lying, the woman is almost always fully represented; but if he is sitting or standing, she is only represented from the waist upwards (...)". This semi-complete, conventional representation of the woman occurs in seventy per cent of fellatio cases; and mostly when the man is sitting. The woman usually holds the man's legs and, less frequently, his sexual organ. The man may be holding or touching her head. There are two cases in which more than two people are present in the fellatio scene; the extras are infants. Evidently, oral-genital contact had a more reserved character than coitus, or than caressing and handling (2). It must be stressed that in Lambayeque and Chimú representations of fellatio, the penis is usually inordinately emphazised.

In representations of fellatio as well as of vaginal and anal coitus, the man wears an impassive expression. His serene face does not reveal the emotion or satisfaction that the fellatio act must have given him, as evidenced by the full erection of his penis. The ecstatic position of his body seems to show that the active person during the act was the woman.

---

(1) Gebhard (8: 32) mentions, however, that self-fellatio was not unknown, as there is "at least one vessel representing an animal in such activity".

(2) "There are no representations —says Gebhard— in which a living woman practises fellatio on a corpse, and in only one, a female corpse is shown practising fellatio on a living man. Fellatio between corpses does not occur".

(3) Larco's statement (1946; 1966: 87) that cunnilingus was practised, is based in an indirect inference "evidenced" by pottery pieces representing women from whose vulva one had to drink. Though we notice that the absence of a representation is not of a definite proof of the absence of a determined sexual practise.

(1) See the percentages estimated by Gebhard (1973, 8: 32) regarding nakedness of partners in fellatio.

(2) The statement refers to the summary established by Gebhard (1973; 8: 31-2) regarding the Moche sample that was analysed.

Fig. 53. Fellatio representation on a Moche sculptured container.
Notice the impassive face of the man (Private Collection).

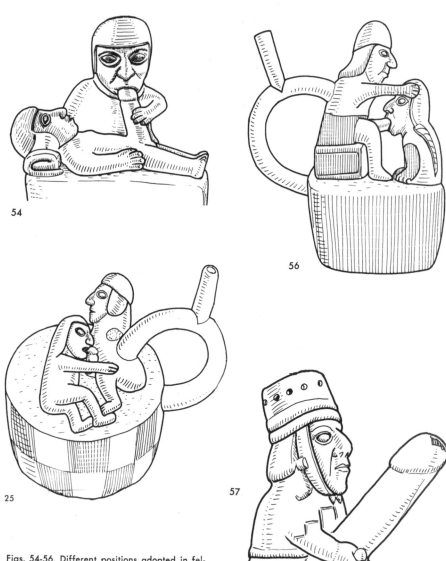

54

56

25

57

Figs. 54-56. Different positions adopted in fellatio. Fig. 57. The author thinks that there may be a relationship between the containers showing persons with a gigantic phallus and fellatio practised as a fertility rite, since one was obliged to place the phallus in one's mouth and drink from it (see Chapter 19). Therefore, he considers that these are not "exhibitionist" or "pornographic", nor representations of "satyrs", as various authors consider them...
(All pieces: N.M.A.A., Lima).

12. *Masturbation*

The manipulation of sexual organs with the hand is present in Moche pottery, as well as in other ceramic styles as we shall see, but always as an exception and cloaked in magic-religious garb, in the almost totality of cases.

The author (KD, 1966: 31) published the hitherto inedited figure of an evident case of masturbation [Fig. 58]. It shows a cadaverous personage, represented in a sculptural way on a Moche vessel, who not only holds but seems to rub his penis. There are even signs of seminal spilling, pictorically represented on the walls of the vessel, where the scene is completed with painted figures. All this leads us to suppose that it was intended to show the subject ejaculating. The example here mentioned shows the classic masturbator, or "onanist": the subject who self masturbates his genital organs.

The fact that masturbators appear in most of the cadaverous cases has been traditionally regarded as an attempt to point out the "damage" to which the "solitary vice" would lead. But the fact that representations exist of cadaverous personages active in other occupations, which have no connection with masturbation, seems to demonstrate the inconsistency of this supposition.

There are other examples in the series of cadaverous beings, seated and with their erect penises in their hands. But here again the "onanist" continues to be the center of a mythical representation. Such is the case of the personage who holds a child against his chest while self-masturbating his genital

Fig. 58. Masturbation scene, practiced by an "animated corpse". This type of representation has been considered as "moralizing": a sign that the "solitary vice" was considered an act which undermined the physical strength of the onanist. Without denying outright that this concept existed in ancient Peru, it is necessary to bear in mind that here this can also be just another act performed by a carcancha —like many others represented— such as dancing which need not be considered as the cause of its skeletic condition... There are on the other, hand, masturbators which obviously are not carcanchas... (Moche, Art Museum, Lima).

organs [Plate XXXI]. On the other hand, there are representations of erected penises without genital manipulation, also with deep mythological content: such is the case of "animated corpses" with erect penis, occupied in playing an antara or Pipes of Pan [Cover].

Finally, in other cases, a cadaverous man is masturbated by a woman; here also the scene seems to be framed in a magic-religious sphere [Fig. 59]. Is this perhaps a type of sexual satisfaction to which the dead men had a right, in the "animated" world of the dead?

But not all the "onanists" are cadaverously represented. In some specimens identified by the author (1), live individuals are represented during masturbation; in both the cases reviewed the expression of the face is half voluptuous and half disgusted. These seem to constitute some of the few examples of masturbators without a magic intent.

──────────

(1) In Mr. and Mrs. Figuerola's collection (Chepén and Lima) and in the former collection of D. Seminario (Piura).

There are also a few examples of masturbation by couples, of living persons, in which the masturbators show clearly an expression of pleasure. This type of representation seems to border on the sphere of erotic caresses, extended to the male genital organ; perhaps, here, it should not be viewed as an act of masturbation, but of caresses which would be followed by a ductual coitus [Fig. 32]. When the woman manipulates the penis, the sexual organ is shown, almost always, in full erection, the gland being visible; its size is usually enormous, specially in Lambayeque and Chimú representations. A singular case [Fig. 60] is one where the protagonist is a woman masturbating a child who lies supine, resting on a sheet (Larco, 1966: 119,

Fig. 59. A woman masturbating a carcancha. The frequency of this type of representation might allude perhaps to a certain impotence attributed to the animated corpse or to other mythical concepts (Moche, N.M.A.A., Lima).

Fig. 60. A case where an adult woman apparently masturbates a child. This scene of probable paidophilia (woman-child) is unique and seems to be involved in magic; it does not therefore belong to the world of pure erotism (Moche IV, R. Larco Herrera Museum, Lima).

and Gebhard, 9: 15). But the act is performed in a ritual rather than a voluptuous atmosphere; especially if one observes the serene face of the woman and her neutral attitude towards the child. There is really no corporal contact, such as can be appreciated in other masturbation representations.

Female masturbation in the form of self-masturbation seems to be absent. But there exists at least one representation of a man caressing a vulva [Fig. 35]. This caressing could well be a prelude which would end with the introduction of the penis into the vulva; however, the known specimen, popularized by Larco, shows that the man is impotent: a prominent breasted eunuch... With regard to female self-masturbation, a curious object from the Albert Fehl-ing Museum, analyzed by the author, must be mentioned. This, due to its phallic shape, could perhaps have been used as a "consoler" or to produce excitation if introduced as a "vulvar paccha" (KD). But perhaps it was only a simple enema applicator; though there is also the supposition that it might have been a defloring instrument (1).

Finally, there are also cases of animals engaged in genital masturbation, but this theme falls within the scope of the chapter on animal sexuality. That is not the case of the Vicús specimen (KD, 1976: 139), masturbating himself; however, this example seems to pertain to the magic sphere [Fig. 62].

_____
(1) See Chapter 20.

Fig. 61. Carcancha, or skeletonized being, holding its erect virile organ. It is not necessarily manipulating its penis in an act of masturbation. (Moche, Private Collection).

Fig. 62. Mythological personage masturbating himself. He has a zoomorphous head and a mouth with protruding teeth represented by grains of corn. (KD, 1976: 141); his arms and hads are ornithomorphous (Vicús, Private Collection).

45

13. *Homosexuality*

In order to halt the wave of popular rumours about the existence of unbridled homosexuality among ancient Peruvians —and particularly among the Moches or Mochicas— which after a preliminary analysis of the collection housed in the National Museum of Lima, the author found to be groundless, in 1963 he wrote the following: "This is contrary to the widely divulged popular version which associates Mochica sexual pottery with homosexual representations" (KD, 1963: 149). And later, clarifying his position: "in everything regarding homosexual practices whose presence in Peru is undeniable, the Mochicas seem not to have liked representing them (...), as can be seen from an analysis of the important collection in the National Museum of Anthropology and Archaeology". (KD, 1966: 28). And, in fact, according to his own evidence and to his surprise, he did not then find even one piece representing a homosexual (1).

Larco (1966: 117) expresses himself in a very similar way, concluding that there were only two representations of "doubtful vases of Vicús pottery" which perhaps might show homosexual cases (2); later he refers to one further pottery specimen, from the Moche culture, about which he also expressed some doubts for reasons of iconographic ambiguity [Fig. 63]. It represents a man, lying on his side, and next to him a skeleton-man also on his side, behind the first; the living subject has his eyes closed, apparently in sound sleep. Larco believed that perhaps it was an act that only took place in an oniric world; perhaps a homosexual dream. This sculptural representation is vague in details, so it is impossible to know whether or not there is anal-genital contact. As one of the two subjects in this representation appears a cadaverous-man or "animated corpse", the scene could well be set within the framework of the series of magic-religious visualizations from the

---

(1) In my note (KD, 1966: 28-29) I added that "according to the verbal information given by the Vice-Director of said museum, only one piece (in the storeroom) reproduces sodomy intercourse, and even this exception under careful analysis is debatable...".

(2) See next Chapter.

Fig. 63. Carcancha lying behind a man, while the latter sleeps. The hypothesis that this is a "homosexual dream" is weak (Moche IV, R. Larco Herrera Museum, Lima).

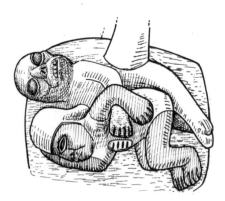

Fig. 64. Unique Moche sculptural container where a homosexual act is clearly represented. See description on Plate XXV (Moche, N.M. A.A. Requisitioned piece).

world of the dead (Chapter 17).

In 1974, during a new examination of the ceramic material on the sexual theme, carried out in the National Museum of Anthropology and Archaeology (3), the author was informed about a Moche container, newly acquired through forfeiture, of much interest in discussions on homosexuality. This piece, in fact, portrays without doubt homosexual intercourse between men [Fig. 64]. In spite of the fact that the container is damaged, there is no doubt whatsoever that it really is an authentic piece and that the ceramist-sculptor wanted to represent eloquently a homosexual scene (KD, 1978: 373, fig. 3).

(3) Thanks to the facilities offered by the Director L. G Lumbreras, Vice-Director H. Rosas, and Official E. Versteylen.

The above mentioned sexual representation in which, as already indicated, two men take part, is at present unique in Moche pottery; it proves that homosexuality was also represented, though rarely, judging by the few examples (KD, 1966: 28). This Moche piece is added to a Vicús representation, which also leaves no room to doubt that a homosexual scene was visualized, but this case will be reviewed in the next chapter.

The above mentioned Moche and Vicús representations contradict Larco's statement (1966: 117-18) that if "there had been sodomy (homosexuality) among the Mochicas, they would have expressed it in their pottery", and that even if "sexual deviation occurs (. . .) such manifestations always distinguished very clearly between the sexes (. . .)". And so Larco concluded by insisting that "(the "degenerates") were never attracted by the same sex. It was always between man and woman. As in heterosexual normality". But later Larco changed his mind, not because of Moche representations, but faced by evidence provided by Vicús pottery (KD, 1976: 141, fig. 2). And as he did not want to set aside his original puritanical hypothesis, he switched the argument to the homosexual nature of this piece, interpreting it as the visualization of coitus between a man and a hermaphrodite (see next chapter).

All that has been said here about Moche pottery, which reproduced in clay what is evidently a homosexual act, constitutes a clear

example that the absence of a representation of a given sexual attitude may be due to several factors: to chance in relation to the discovery or destruction of pieces over the years, and even at the hands of modern "iconoclasts" (1); to a dislike of representing certain acts; and, even, to the presence of taboos when portraying certain sexual attitudes. Therefore, the absence of iconographic evidence is not necessarily equivalent to the absence of a habit, in this case, homosexuality, which is a practice that appears universally and whose origins are lost in time. And, by extension, neither is rarity of representations such as the piece already mentioned (KD, 1977: 373) —here reproduced in color (2)— a criterion on which to base a statement about whether homosexuality was wide spread or limited during the Moche period. . .

Finally, with Larco (1966: 118) and Gebhard (1973: 9: 27) we state that female homosexuality, or "lesbianism", was not shown in pottery, though we do not agree with those specialists that such activity was "completely absent (because) there are no specimens that insinuate it".

---

(1) This "patriotic" attitude of trying to erase historical stains is testified by Valdizán, as M. A. Denegri has pointed out (1977: 4-7). Valdizán (1915: 85) mentions, in fact, the presence of ceramic pieces with "scenes of sodomy or pederasty" adding that "a misunderstood modesty has led many collectors to destroy them . . .".

---

(2) Thanks to photographs taken specially for the author, by Dr. R. Shady de Rosas, in 1974.

14. *Hermaphrodites and Pseudo-Hermaphrodites*

In cultures prior to Moche, Virú and Vicús, representations can be found which portray beings endowed with two sexes, or hermaphrodites.

The presence of a Vicús container [Fig. 65], in which two men are shown, one of them penetrating the other per anum with his virile organ, was reported by Larco as an example of a hermaphrodite (KD, 1976: 141, fig. 2). The individual taking the part of the passive or female homosexual, allowing the active homosexual to insert his phallus in an anal coitus, is shown holding his penis in his hand. His inactive sexual organ, thus held, naturally appears flaccid and small compared with that of his partner: it is held to one side so that it will not be in the way during the homosexual act, since the act took place with the passive homosexual lying supine. This representation allows us, nevertheless, to assume a critical attitude toward the hermaphrodite nature which Larco attributes to the passive homosexual, since it could well be just a scene between homosexuals.

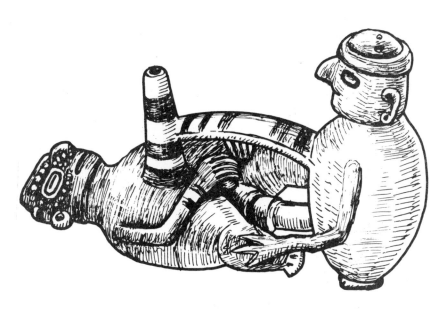

Fig. 65. This piece has been described as a representation of a homosexual act between a man and a hermaphrodite. However, it is impossible to determine positively the hermaphroditic nature of the passive homosexual (Vicús, Private Collection).

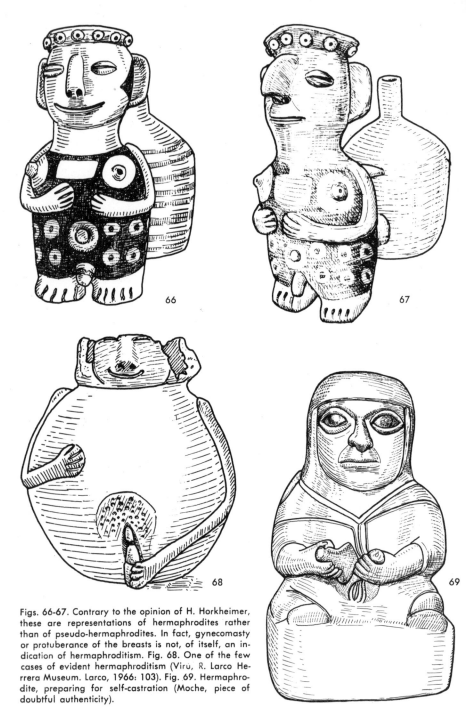

Figs. 66-67. Contrary to the opinion of H. Horkheimer, these are representations of hermaphrodites rather than of pseudo-hermaphrodites. In fact, gynecomasty or protuberance of the breasts is not, of itself, an indication of hermaphroditism. Fig. 68. One of the few cases of evident hermaphroditism (Viru, R. Larco Herrera Museum. Larco, 1966: 103). Fig. 69. Hermaphrodite, preparing for self-castration (Moche, piece of doubtful authenticity).

An anthropomorphous Virú vase ("Gallinazo") with a demaged top section, made known by Larco and divulged by Gebhard (1973, 7: 23) is the only representation that portrays a case of evident hermaphroditism [Fig. 68]. All duobt is dispersed here, because the ceramist shows now the individual obviously tries with his hand to insert his penis into his own vulva. Gebhard (1973, 7: 24) mentions that he knows only one other case of hermaphrodite representation: a Moche figure where the individual is shown amputating his penis. We do not know this specimen; but we do know one, of the same style, kept in the National Museum of Anthropology and Archaeology (Lima) which has inspired many good quality forgeries, representing scenes of self-castration [Fig. 69].

Besides the cases quoted, mention must be made of a group of Vicús anthropomorphous representations of standing figures of human beings, apparently hermaphrodites, specially judging by the secondary sexual characters with which they are shown [Figs. 66, 67]. In fact, these subjects, modeled in clay and "dressed" with tattoos, are endowed with a penis as well as with breasts. But again in this case some doubts arise. The prominent breasts, whose nipples have orifices from which to pour liquid, could well correspond to congenital homosexuals: effeminate from birth with signs of gynecomasty, that is an exaggerated prominence of the breasts, and, for that same reason, not necessarily genuine hermaphrodites... We must add that such representations do not display any erotic content;

they seem to be truly linked to the magic-religious context.

15. *Bestiality or Zooerasty*

Sexual relations between human beings and animals is the theme of myths and folklore fables, and is world-wide; the *Kinsey Report* mentions that practices of zooerasty (1) are more frequent than has been so far acknowledged.

This is not the place to comment on those representations of deep magic-religious content, raised to divine planes, where anthropomorphous beings are shown joined in an amorous fashion to zoomorphous beings, or even having intercourse with them; the same mythical character noted in these representations leads us to consider them as a special series which will be examined in the next chapter. Iconography of purely animal sexuality will also be the subject of a separate review.

The various coital representations in the Vicús culture where a woman's body adopts the form of a quadruped [Fig. 70] must not, properly speaking, be considered as examples of intercourse of humans with beasts (2). It is seen that in these women who pose as quadrupeds, the human figure predominates over the animal one, for which reason we must presume that the hybridism they show is mythological.

---

(1) Synonym for bestiality, discussed and divulged by M. A. Denegri (1977).

(2) Gebhard (1973: 2: 27) only mentions cases belonging to the Moche culture similar to the ones commented on here.

Fig. 70. Coitus where the woman assumes the face and zoomorphous position of a quadruped (KD, 1969: 277). Vicús/Vicús. Private Collection.

Nevertheless the mythical content is not raised here to the high spheres present in the figures mentioned in the next chapter that are truly mythological. Thus, while the woman, with a human head, adopts the position of a quadruped, the man, standing and copulating her from behind, shows contours that are definitely anthropomorphous. But it is surprising that both the man and the woman have very pronounced noses, which the author interprets as an ornithomorphic allusion (KD, 1969, 1974: 344). But the "birdbeak" nose does not appear only in personages sexually active: it is extended, in Vicús, as a *leitmotif* in the majority of anthropomorphous beings shown in the pottery of that culture and its discussion, therefore, is beyond the scope of this theme. In the Vicús examples of intercourse between man and woman who adopt the body and position of quadrupeds it is finally not possible to define if they are vaginal or per anum coitus, due to the vagueness of details given by the ceramist.

Going straight to the subject, it can be said that from the XVI Century, chroniclers like Cieza (1553) and other written testimonies of that time, allude to evident cases of zooerasty practised by the natives. On the other hand, J. J. v. Tschudi, a scholar who lived at the end of last Century, laid the ground work for that version, widely publicised in the XX Century, saying that the habit of copulating with llamas was and always will be a widespread habit among the natives of the Peruvian highlands. However, without for a moment intending to present it as a proof

to the contrary —that is the hypothesis of the absence of trace of zooerasty with llamas in ancient Peru, and which, according to Villavicencio (1942: 125), might

Fig. 71. Aiapaec holds by the hair a woman who carries her son at her back. It is impossible to state, definitively, whether this is a mythological scene of sexual content in which violence is applied (Moche).

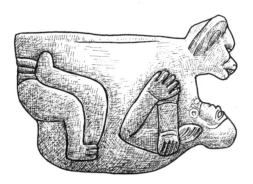

Fig. 72. Probable representation of pseudo-zoophilia. The male in fact is human in everything related to its body; only its head is zoomorphous and seems to suggest the shape of a dog's head. Larco (1966: 145) states that it is "a woman, copulating with a vampire". It could well be a "masked" subject, according to several other iconographic examples of the same style (Moche. R. Larco Herrera Museum).

53

Fig. 73. Unique scene apparently representing a case of bestiality. The position of the woman is the one she would usually adopt during coitus (Moche, Art Museum of Chicago. From a photograph by Gebhard, 1973).

have been total yesterday as well as today— the author must point out that he has so far not found any archaeological representation showing human intercourse with llamas. Neither has Larco, nor Gebhard. This apparent contradiction with reference to the information of the XVI Century, has been clarified by the investigations carried out on that point by M.A. Denegri (1977). This scholar has found quotations in works of Tello (1909: 394) and Valdizán (1915: 82), from which it is apparent that in those days there were pottery pieces representing cases of coupling with llamas, in possession of museums and collections in Lima and he has ascertained that these were destroyed by "cultured" persons, due to a mistaken patriotism, in an effort to erase proofs that showed the presence of a practice considered as abominable. Tello says, in fact, that the habit of zooerasty with llamas was demonstrated by the "great frequency" of such representations; and Valdizán comments that the debated "matter about bestiality among primitive Peruvians" is

54

cleared up by the "existence of pottery pieces". The absence today of ceramic pieces in State museums and collections in Lima, permits us to establish that, at a later period, lovers of a past free from historical taints, faithful to their "commitment" as consumated patriots have systematically destroyed those pieces...

It is certain that, at present, there is only one available Moche pottery piece, which apparently shows a "bestiality" scene [Fig. 73]. And it is not precisely a zooerastic relation with a llama. Neither is it, as might be supposed "a priori" a scene where a man appears to be copulating with a beast. A woman enters the scene: she is lying "knocked down" by a dog (1). The representation was reported and commented on by Larco (1966: 31), but this scholar was sceptical in considering it as a portrayal of a "bestiality" scene; he thought rather that it might simply be the figure of a woman attacked by a dog... But the scene

_____

(1) Piece in the Chicago Art Museum.

shows the woman supine, naked, with her legs open and the genitals represented in detail, even the clitoris; and the large dog stands over her, with its forefeet on her shoulders, while its hind feet are posed on her thighs, as if "holding the woman's legs apart". Moreover, though "its penis is broken", the dog points the stump "towards the vulva, which seems to contain a piece of the penis". According to Gebhard (1973, 9: 22), the fact "that the woman has her legs open, the detail with which her genitals have been represented, and the evident tumescence of the dog's penis", leads one to think that it could well be a sexual scene. But the presence of overtones of the votive and mythological character of the scene should also be noted; the larger, almost surrealistic scale, on which the animal is portrayed, may perhaps substantiate this.

16. *Sexuality among divine beings and the upper hierarchy of the mythical sphere*

In almost all sexual representations produced in ancient Peru, a background of magic religious origin can be discovered, which is expressed with sometimes more and sometimes less intensity. Apart from the iconographic groups analyzed so far, most of which appear to be imbued with the votive import already mentioned, it is possible to isolate one more category of sexual representations. This refers to those portrayals where one or both protagonists of a scene can be found to be not only endowed with a magic religious character, but in fact typify the highest hierarchy of religious beliefs; in some cases they seem

even to incarnate the very image of some god [Figs. 1, 78, 79].

It is necessary to stress that the mythical content of the specimens included in this group is not only deep, but it prevails over every genital-erotic expectancy. Even in the examples of coital representations, the divine character of the coitus is quite clearly insinuated, and seems to have no other purpose than to show a natural and perhaps propitiatory act of procreation. An illustration [Fig. 80], of what has been said is the scene showing an agglomeration of potato seeds which is "fecundated" in a coitai act... In other cases, as in the theme of the "Tello Obelisk", the deity's capacity of fecundation-creation is shown separate from the properly coital context, seen in the figure of a phallus in ejaculation [Fig. 2].

Phallus in ejaculation (Chavín divinity — "Obelisco Tello", Museum of Anthropology and Archaeology, Lima).

Generally speaking, it is suprising that there are few representations of sexual acts in which beings of a truly divine quality take part.

Scenes of caressing and amorous contact between humans and animals —which, due to their clearly mythological context must not be confused with representations of zooerasty— as well as scenes that obviously show coitus by divine beings apart from being imbued with a deep votive significance, indicate other characteristics that should be noted: the sexual act on the divine plane is not framed within the canons of heterosexuality, that is to say, it takes place between a man and a woman; oral coitus is absent, as well as masturbation or genital manipulation (whether "onanism" or in groups) in order to stimulate the libido; cases of heterosexual per anum coitus ("sodomy") are not represented in copulating deities, contrary to the opinion —neither detailed nor illustrated— given in Larco's book (1966: 101).

It can be said, finally, that among the representations selected as types of the groups we are studying —basically Moche and Huari-Pativilca— which will be analyzed later, there are some that, due to a lack of eloquence in figuration, should not necessarily be considered as sexual visualizations on the

divine plane, but rather as mythological evocations, free from sexual content [Fig. 75].

THE "PERUVIAN LEDA". Due to the suggestion it offers in relation to Greek mythology, of the love between Leda and a swan, in which a divinity is incarnated, we classify as a "Peruvian Leda" representations exhibited in the Larco Museum and in other collections, where a woman is shown together with a bird [Fig. 74]. The protagonists of this scene seems to melt in an intimate corporal but not coital contact: they are shown front view, their bodies touching at the side and they are embracing each other around the shoulders; both rest their heads, reclining them one against the other in an amor-

Fig. 74. Union of a bird with a human being. Due to the position of both figures, and to the fact that they are leaning against each other, it could be deduced that it is a love scene within a mythical context. Published by Larco (1966: 78, 144), as a "vessel having approximately the shape of a fruit" (Moche, R. Larco Herrera Museum, Lima).

Fig. 75. Aiapaec mounts on a human-shaped bird, who seems to hold him by the hands. Mythological scene, not necessarily sexual (Moche, Private Collection. Drawing: Martha Kauffmann Doig).

ous gesture; the woman's hand is placed on the bird's genital zone. The bird equals in size the anthropomorphous figure —which we believe to be that of a woman— but its only human characteristic are the feet, transformed into legs. The "woman" wears a sort of cap which seems to be a simulation of the ornithomorphous head of her "consort". The artist does not bring out any details, so that a "fusion" of both beings occurs; this leads one to perceive in the scene, an atmosphere of love but with no signs of voluptuosity. If the personage we have been considering as a woman should prove to be a man and if the bird represents a woman, the scene could be correlated to the myth of the "guacamayos" or bird women —one of whom is seduced by a survivor of the "flood"— and about which Molina informs us (MS, XVI C.). In any case, we repeat, this is not a representation of zooerasty.

Fig. 76. Bird copulating with a person, or perhaps, using him as a boat (Chimú, N.M.A.A., Lima).

AIAPAEC MOUNTED ON A BIRD. Another Moche mythical scene which also deals with a bird and a human being, is that in which one of the personages is Aiapaec (1), the supreme Moche deity [Fig. 75]. He is seen mounted on a large bird of prey, perhaps a sea eagle (KD, 1976: 164). But, though the scene at first sight seems to suggest that Aiapaec is copulating, the ambiguity of the representation does not permit us to determine

whether in fact the intention was to represent an act of coupling or merely a scene where the deity appears flying on the bird's back; or it might reproduce a lost chapter or a variation of the Ñaymlap myth, which, archaeologically, can

(1) Name given by Larco to the Moche deity of human shape but with a tiger's mouth. The name is equivalent to the concept of "supreme being" and is taken from Carrera's *Grammar* (1644).

58

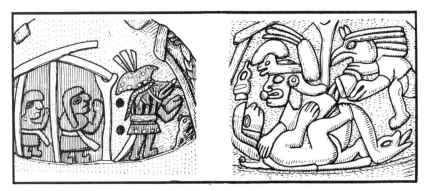

Fig. 77. Aiapaec copulating, while several women wait their turn
(Scene figured in high relief, on a Moche container; A. Fehling Museum, Lima).

now be traced in the Moche culture (KD, 1963; 1964; 1978: 495-99).

MYTHICAL BIRD LYING ON A HUMAN BEING. A third example in which a human being and a bird take part, is that of a container in the National Museum of Anthropology and Archaeology (Lima); it is probably of a late period and comes from the North Coast [Fig. 76]. Here an enormous bird rides on a human being, who is lying face down, and seems to be firmly held by the four-fingered, ornithomorphous feet. At first sight mythical intercourse seems to be expressed in this piece. However, the fact that the human personage does not clearly show a female face, and that its body is barely sketched, opens up a second possible interpretation of this scene: perhaps it is a bird using a human being as a "boat"...

AIAPAEC IN MULTIPLE COPULATIONS. A Moche scene, obviously sexual-mythical, is one representing the deity Aiapaec copulating with a woman who is totally human [Fig. 77]. While this takes place, other women wait their

turn... Aiapaec is helped by two masked personages and by other minor servants. One of them, with a bird's head, seems to pour over the couple (on to Aiapaec's back) some liquid from the vessel held in his hands; meanwhile, the other senior servant guards a hut where women patiently wait their turn to be fecundated by the deity (1). Aiapaec appears dressed during this act of ceremonial copulation and is still wearing his breeches, held by a belt terminating in the shape of a snake; the woman on the contrary stands naked.

DEITIES COPULATING. Mention should be made of scenes where deities of both sexes are shown having intercourse [Figs. 1, 78]. This type of representation is depicted with outlines in relief, drawn on the walls of jars coming from the Pativilca-Casma area; from their style, they belong to the twilight of the Tiahuanaco-Huari Horizon ("Pachacamac" influ-

---

(1) The Moche specimen analyzed belongs to the Albert Fehling Museum (Lima). There are other jars with scenes similar to the one described. (KD, 1976: 161).

Fig. 78. Coitus in the heavenly sphere, with a wide display of mythological symbols (Pativilca container, of Pachacamac-Huari influence. N.M.A.A. Publ. Carrión 1959).

Fig. 79. Two representations of the same scene, on a Pativilca container, of Pachacamac-Huari influence, here characterized as the Peruvian version of "Adam and Eve in Paradise" (N.M.A.A., Lima).

Fig. 80. Mythological personage "copulating" an agglomeration of potatoes, which together take the shape of a woman in a supine position (Moche. Piece divulged by Tello, 1938).

ence). The author examined the specimens in the National Museum of Anthropology and Archaeology, Lima (KD, 1969: 432, 514). The representations to which we refer show the two divinities copulating. They are drawn within a larger context, formed by divers subsidiary figures (2). The divine couple nevertheless occupies the central area, surrounded by scenery that seems to represent the heavenly world. The copulating deities emit rays, which usually end in snake heads; perhaps they allude to the resplandent nature of the divine personages.

THE PRIMITIVE COUPLE. In the same archaeological style as the representations just mentioned are scenes where the central motif is a human couple, man and woman, both naked, holding hands and sitting face to face [Fig. 79]. From them are "born" branches in which monkeys appear, always supposing that the artist did not intend to represent a central tree

beneath which the couple appears seated. It should be borne in mind here that the couple does not necessarily represent deities: it could well be a Peruvian version of the theme "Adam and Eve in Paradise". Therefore, the scene we refer to belongs in any case, to the high hierarchy of the mythical sphere, probably linked to concepts referring to acts of creation.

PAPA-MAMA COPULATION. Representations where an agglomeration of potatoes, which has assumed the shape of a woman in a supine position, is copulated by a being of human form also belong to the purely mythical sphere [Fig. 80]. The man depicted is a mortal and even if he is sumptuously dressed, the whole scene can only be classified as a copulation in the high sphere of myth. The female figure which rises from the agglomeration of potatoes could be the "papamama" or minor deity, responsible for the abundance or shortage of this tuber.

17. *Sexuality in the world of "animated skeletons" or carcanchas*

Sexuality is present not only in the world of living persons; it continues after death. This concept should not cause surprise if one considers the idea of a "life" beyond the grave and the consequent cult of the dead professed by ancient Peruvians even before the days of "high culture" [Fig. 81]. There is no doubt that the "uco-pacha", or world of the dead, was represented as a place in which "life" continued, with "carcanchas" or "living" skeletal beings [Fig. 83]. But the carcancha also enters or makes his presence felt in the world of the living, and even keeps in touch with living beings as shown by iconography which exists on that subject. Here again it is the Moche culture which consolidates practically all the information.

Fig. 81. Sexuality is projected into the world of the dead. The mummified bodies "guaranteed" the life in the other world; they were carefully wrapped in clothes and placed in tombs, with vessels containing food and beverages, and even with women who were sacrified specially ("necropomposity" — C. Araníbar). In this mummy we can notice that it was intended to mummify the genitals as was in fact done. Notice the mummification of the prepuce (Art Museum, Lima).

Fig. 82. Dance of men and women Carcanchas. In the center, Aiapaec or his delegate (Pub.: Ch. Mead).

It is interesting to note that a considerable part of all the iconography relating to the carcanchas is tinged with sexual elements. But there are scenes that seem to evoque only orgies animated by drink where men and women, holding hands, take part and the deity Aiapaec —or the "chaman carcancha" who is his incarnation— appears in a trance [Fig. 82]. The artist represents the dead as carcanchas; that it so say, as only partially skeletons, perhaps in order to endow them with dynamism, and perhaps due to the fact of imagining the dead as "living". The various scenes, painted on the walls of a jar or represented in terracotta figures, perhaps take place at night, when the spirits protected by darkness appear to be more dynamic... (KD, 1978: 361). Aiapaec does not always appear in painted scenes, but the carcancha's clothes show us that earthly hierarchies continued in the world beyond: carcancha-musicians with Pipes of Pan, quenas or drums enliven the macabre festivities, while jars, shown next to the skeletonized beings, allude to the beverages they are drinking...

Among the painted iconography, there is one sexual scene between male and female carcanchas, which is of special interest [Fig. 83]. One of the animated skeletons, naked, embraces a skull-woman, pointing towards her his half-erect virile organ, which he holds in his hand; all the personages seem to look upwards, where a masturbator, also a cadaver, sculpturally depicted, is apparently having an orgasm and spills his semen over the carcanchas (KD, 1966: 31; 1978: 373). In the chapter on masturbation, we have reached the conclusion that the presence of carcanchas in masturbation acts allows us to assert that, contrary to popular belief, the masturbator is not skeletonized because of such a practice...

More numerous sexual representations of the world of the dead have been made in plastic form. Apart from the onanist already mentioned and other versions on the same subject, the Mochicas showed scenes in which men and women carcanchas take part, as well as men carcanchas and living women; the couples are seated, arms around each others shoulders,

Fig. 83. Sexual dance in the world of the dead. The actors look upwards, where a masturbator ejaculates his semen (Art Museum, Lima).

while the woman caresses or masturbates her consort [Figs. 84, 86, 87]. It would be venturesome to speculate on the meaning of these representations, as many explanations could be found. What seems evident is that the carcanchas, besides masturbating in couples —sometimes accompanied by a third inactive carcancha— kissing each other with the tongue and practising onanism and self-excitement without genital manipulation, are not shown copulating, save for rare exceptions (1). Nor are they performing acts of "sodomy" or fellatio (2). Homosexual scenes in the world of the carcanchas are unknown; the case of the skele-

tonized being, apparently a man resting behind a sleeping youngster, is the subject of discussion; as was seen, it is impossible to define whether or not there is a sexual act, because of the vagueness of the sculpture (3).

(1) Gebhard (1973, 9: 10) only mentions two cases of coital representations between a living woman and a male corpse. Living men do not appear copulating with female corpses.

(2) Gebhard (1973, 8: 32) mentions one case in which a female corpse has fellatio relations with a living man.

(3) Larco (1966) considers that it could be a homosexual dream.

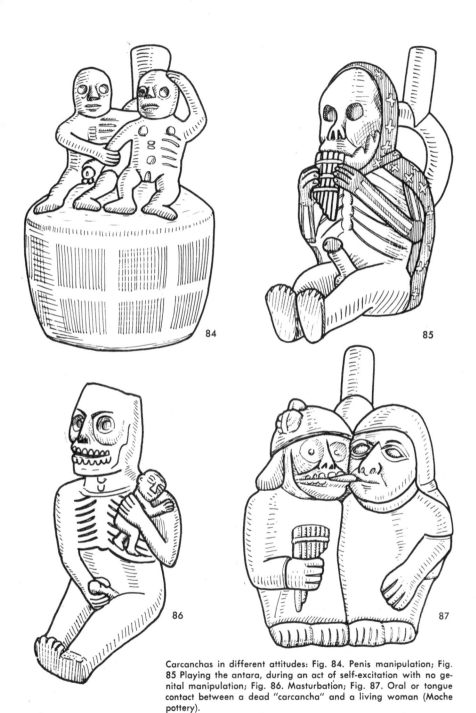

Carcanchas in different attitudes: Fig. 84. Penis manipulation; Fig. 85 Playing the antara, during an act of self-excitation with no genital manipulation; Fig. 86. Masturbation; Fig. 87. Oral or tongue contact between a dead "carcancha" and a living woman (Moche pottery).

Fig. 88. Human-shaped phallus, or anthropophallus (Moche, N. M.A.A.).

18. *Camouflaged anthropophalluses and anthropovulvas*

The phalluses and vulvas that have been sculptorically depicted though camouflaged as persons, obviously belong to the magic sphere; they appear particularly in Moche pottery. Magic sexuality includes other aspects that will be separately reviewed; for example, a case contrary to this one, where the genitals are shown openly or even in an unrestrained way. We

can say, in any case, that the objects we mention in this chapter should not be classified as "phallic cult", because, among other reasons, the "camouflaged genitals" are not only male...

Nevertheless most of the "camouflaged genitals" that appear in the series are phalluses and only very seldom is the vulva figured. Real anthropophalluses —or "phallic persons" according to Gebhard's nomenclature— represent human beings, men who are generally kneeling, crowned by a strange

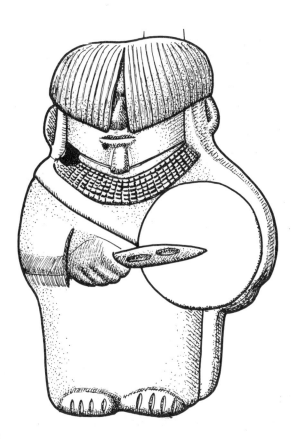

Fig. 89. Human-shaped vulva, or anthropovulva (Moche, R. Larco Herrera Museum).

headdress, or "cap" in which can be discovered —but only by examining the sculptural piece from certain angles— the representation of the penis gland [Fig. 88]. Judging by some obvious cases, the whole human body bears the contours of the virile organ; specially at the back of the anthropophallus which appears plain and slightly curved. These jars are considered by Larco to be moralizers because "in them, the sexual obsession of the personage is symbolized, and because its face is very marked by libertinism". (Larco, 1966: 54, 144).

The anthropovulva, or person in which a camouflaged vulva appears, maintains as a whole, a human silhouette, somewhat similar to that of the anthropophalluses [Fig. 89]. In the specimen in the Larco Herrera Museum —as well as in that of the National Museum of Anthropology— a woman with a strange hair style is shown; she is playing a tinya or small drum. The hair of the personage covers her face down to her nose, and it

Fig. 90. Captured warrior, whose hair is dressed giving a phallic allusion (Vicús, Private Collection).

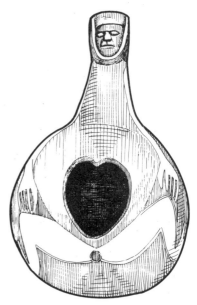

Fig. 91. Toaster on which a woman's body is drawn, the handle alluding to a phallus (Moche, R. Larco Herrera Museum).

is carefully combed and symmetrically cut. But it is above all the center parting of the hair, combed downwards, together with the tip of the nose, sticking out from the hair like a clitoris, which helps to suggest that the intention was to show a vulva. Naturally, as the female genitals are represented as appearing in the head, there is no additional sexual suggestion in the clothed body of the personage.

Also belonging to the "camouflaged phallus" sphere, are certain early Moche and Vicús jars showing personages with hair dressed so as to resemble a mushroom-shaped figure, which, undoubtedly, is an allusion to the gland; but it should be noted that the rest of the individual's body does not show sexual signs [Figs. 90, 92]. Consequently,

Fig. 92. Captive warrior, with a phallic handle (R. Larco Herrera Museum).

they are not authentic "anthropo-phalluses". They are rather persons who arrange their hair to imitate the shape of the penis gland, thereby symbolizing their physical strength and perhaps their potency; it is also symptomatic in this sense, that the individuals who wear the "phallic hair dress" adopt warrior's poses.

The toasters from the Moche period also fall within the sphere of camouflaged phalluses. They have a handle which, probably by suggestion, takes more or less covertly the figure of a phallus [Fig. 91]. The glands of these phalluses imitate the shape of a small human head.

We mention finally that there are also versions of Moche anthropo-phallus sculptured in stone coming from the Bolivian high tableland [Figs. 93, 94].

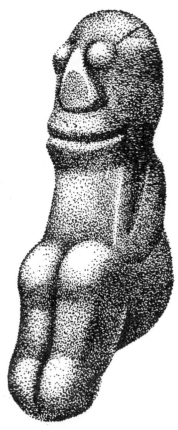

Figs. 93-94. Two small anthropomorphous monoliths. The one on the left has a cap with phallic allusion (camouflaged phallus); the one on the right judging by its style, belongs to the other one, though it does not wear the phallic cap (Titicaca Region, Art Museum. The height of the monolith on the right is 19 cm.).

19. *Anthropomorphous jars, endowed with genitals for drinking*

There is a group of Moche pottery specimens whose particularity is to represent sculptures of men and of women also, endowed with prominent genitals, perforated in region of the meatus or vulva, respectively, as if they were to be drunk from... These objects must not be considered as representations of sexual exhibitionism [Figs. 57, 105], nor confused with the previous group of anthroposexual beings. The latter lack the particularity of having an orifice from which the liquid could run out.

Except for a sub-group (1) the containers on which we are commenting, were in the first place, used for drinking directly from the genitals, as will be seen in detail further on, and not for pouring liquid, for instance for besprinkling an object of worship. Thus, we must discard the possibility that in the case of the phalluses they were used for introduction in the vagina, just as we must discard the idea that the female counterparts have been made for use in male masturbation. We must also say, in this introductory note, that the author is in disagreement in considering these vases as "humorous"; rather he considers that this appreciation is derived from a contemporary view and that these objects belong to the fertility cult.

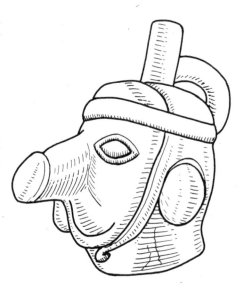

Fig. 95. Head, with lips and nose transformed into genitals (Moche, Private Collection).

Even more correctly, to the sexual magic directed to fertility. There are, however some objects that have perhaps a joking or humorous explanation, within an erotic context, if they do not also possess a certain magic sense: I refer to pieces such as that representing a man, with his nose transformed into a phallus [Fig. 95], or to the few anthropomorphous figures showing very large phalluses without an orifice, that is, lacking the function of being used for drinking directly from the genital, like a piece from the Albert Fehling Museum [Fig. 98]. The sample of libation vases from the genitals, examined in this chapter, is on the other hand relatively too small to permit the assumption that they might have had just a humorous character, because this quality would have shown in their

---

(1) I refer to the containers that show naked women, lying face upwards, with their legs open. These containers have stirrup handles, which start on one side of the vulva.

70

"popularity" (1). It can be inferred finally, that anthropomorphous jars provided with genitals to drink from, would contain beverages, and not simply water; perhaps beverages with fertility powers, real or magic, as a recourse to produce fertility in men and women, and, through this, in the whole world of nature. In other words, a kind of "sexual paccha" of a special category as regards their shape and even perhaps the way were handled. (2).

Even when the group of sexual pottery we refer to is basically made up of Moche pottery objects and anthropomorphous male and female figures are referred to (3), it is necessary to consider within the series those Vicús containers of simple spherical bodies, but crowned by a beak (or beaks) which represent an erect penis, generally large, provided with an orifice from which to drink, very specially those with a double phallus which forced

one to drink inevitably from the virile organ itself [Fig. 100].

The classic anthropomorphous Moche container endowed with a phallus to drink from [Fig. 104], represents a man with a lively expression —sometimes a being whose head has been transformed into a skull— who with one or both hands, holds his phallus, enormous in relation to the size of his body; the gland, exposed, showing its orifice. Liquid was poured from the largest opening of the container, located in the skull region. What is surprising is the presence of small orifices, set all round the largest opening, which, no doubt, were made in order to indicate, in a practical way, that this was not the place to drink from, as through these orifices the liquid would run out in an uncontrolled fashion hopelessly soaking whoever dared to drink from that larger opening instead of from the phallus itself.

Probably, it was necessary to in-

---

(1) It is interesting to notice the presence of an assistant to the deity Aiapaec who during the latter's copulation, seems to pour liquid from a jar over the deity's buttocks; however, the container shows no signs of portraying an anthropomorphous jar with genitals. And this confirms on the other hand all that has been said about the objects we refer to being used for pouring and not for drinking.

(2) The common "paccha" is a container which has an orifice or channel with no sexual figures [Fig. 27]; excepting special cases, such as some "phallus pacchas" [Fig. 96]. The objects we refer to in this chapter could well be classified as "sexual pacchas". But also the paccha that does not assume the form of a penis is somehow linked with the theme of sexuality within the context of fertility. It is presumed that they were objects of worship from which water or chicha was poured in ritual acts. Carrión (1955) who has dedicated a large

and valuable monograph to this theme, considers the paccha as a central instrument in the worship of water. That is to say, in what is understood as rain magic, whose ultimate aim was to ensure the fertility of the fields... But the paccha was isolated, originally, among archaeological testimonies, by Joyce (1923), with the help of a drawing from the beginning of the XVIII Century, which appears in Frezier's work (1716, Fig. IX) and which still survived as an object of worship in Talhuanaco (Chile). The paccha is defined by Ludovico Bertonio (1602) as a "fountain that pours water through some pipe" and also as a "wooden instrument from which chicha in a hollow" was drunk as a pastime. The latter characterization is specially intersting in order to understand the objects examined in this chapter and which, in a general way, we have classified as "sexual pacchas".

(3) We do not know of vessels like the ones mentioned above, corresponding to animal shapes.

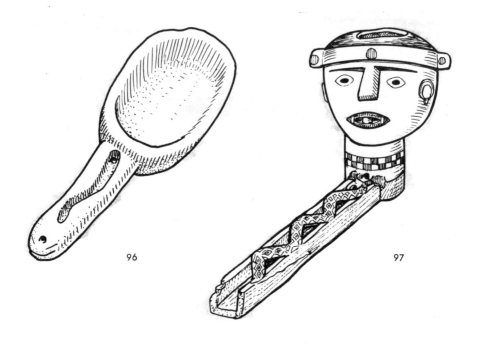

96

97

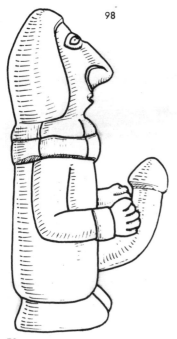

98

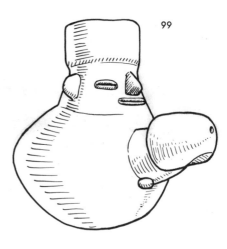

99

Fig. 96. "Paccha" types: Stone paccha, simulating a phallus (Art Museum). Fig. 97. Inca wooden paccha, probably colonial with no direct phallic allusion (Art Museum). Fig. 98. Simulation of a Paccha, as the penis has no meatus (Moche, A. Fehling Museum). Pag. 99. Sexual paccha, destined for use in "artificial fellatio" (Moche, Private Collection).

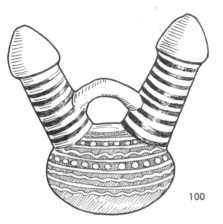

Fig. 100. Types of "paccha": Non anthropomorphous sexual paccha, formed by two phalluses from which to drink (Vicús, Private Collection).

Fig. 101. Pottery object destined for use in "artificial fellation". Fig. 102. Anthropomorphous sexual paccha which forced anyone who drank from it to place his mouth on the vulva (Moche, Art Museum). Fig. 103. Anthropomorphous paccha with no direct sexual allusion (Recuay, N.M.A.A., Lima).

troduce the phallus into the mouth, thus committing an act of "artificial fellatio". But we consider that this designation does not properly define the function fulfilled by these objects; which was not to serve as a fellatory recreation, but to serve as containers of some substance to be ingested within a magic context. The very function of these objects explains, on the other hand, the enormously large phallus in relation to the size of the body. These anthropomorphous pitchers are relatively small, so, had the phallus been on the same scale as the person represented, its size would have very tiny, and inappropriate to drink from... For this same reason, we consider of no validity the supposition that men shown with giant phalluses represented "satyrs". Would men also have drunk from these phallic containers?

On the other hand, the classic female version of the object described above, is that of a container

73

104

105

Fig. 104. Male and female "paccha": Anthropomorphous paccha with a prominent phallus from which to drink; only in a certain manner simulating an act of fellatio. The exaggerated size of the phallus corresponds to its function; the author does not agree with the idea of classifying this type of representations as a simple "showing", nor as a sculpture of "satyrs" (Moche, N.M.A.A.). Fig. 105. Plate with double bottom on which the figure of a woman is drawn. The vulva forms the opening to the lower container, and from it poured the liquid when one drank from it... (Moche, N.M.A.A., Lima).

which, when raised to the mouth for the purpose of drinking, forced the person to drink the liquid running out of the vulva [Fig. 105]. In order to obtain this effect, a double-bottomed clay container was made; in the upper part, visible, appears in relief a woman lying face upwards, with her legs open, arms extended, and a vulva-hole connected to the lower compartment, from which, inevitably, the liquid flowed when anyone

drank from the container. There are variations of this type of sexual pottery such as a jar [Fig. 102] representing a woman, with her legs bent and open: the liquid flows from the vulva orifice so that in order to drink one was forced to touch the vulvar region directly with the lips (1).

20. *Ceramic Phalluses for Vaginal Penetration*

In the preceding chapter, through the examination of the vessels representing personages endowed with large phalluses, the conclusion is reached that such containers were made to drink from, taking some probably fecundating substances into the mouth for purposes of magic. In fact nothing seems to

(1) Larco (1966) considers that this type is a proof that *cunnilingus* was practised among the Moches. Without rejecting the presence of this practice, the archaeological "proof" turns out to be weak. It is that these objects, as already explained, do not seem to have served as a fellatory recreation, properly speaking.

74

indicate that, in such representations, the purpose of the erect virile organ might have been to introduce it into the vagina, less still of having served as the "consolers" of those times.

Only one pottery piece must be separated from the group of human figures endowed with an erect penis already described, not only because of its shape but due to the different function it must have fulfilled. We refer to a rare object [Fig. 106 + Plate XXXIV] that the author had the opportunity of examining in the Albert Fehling Museum (Lima). In one of the extreme sectors the shape of a phallus is noticed, slightly conical in shape, having the gland disclosed and an orifice in the meatus region. The phallus rises from a figure of conic form and ends in a sort of cylindrical-shaped handle.

The conic figure, adorned with striae, is shown at such a distance from the gland that it is possible to notice a flange which would prevent the simulated virile organ from entering further than it should, in case it were thrust into the vagina or the anus.

The object referred to could be considered as an irrigator to be introduced into the vagina for the application of curative substances, magic fertilizers or perhaps stimulants. The author believes it is not a medical instrument for applying enemas by the anus, because of the "natural" size of the penis, and above all due to the protuberance alluding to the gland, both of which would be awkward for anal penetration; also, in view of the presence of a flange, it does not seem to have been meant to be placed in the mouth for drinking. It might have served in deflowering rites, as is insinuated by the slightly conic shape of the penis the presence of the protuberance of the gland, free of the prepuce and the flange to avoid a lesion in the uterus. It is unlikely to have been instrument made specially for female masturbation; which does not mean that this practice was absent.

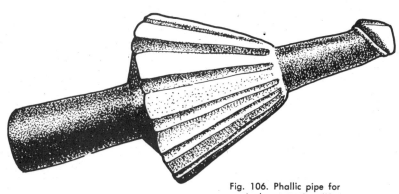

Fig. 106. Phallic pipe for vaginal penetration (Moche, A. Fehling Museum).

21. Phallic Cult?

Commentaries about objects dealing with sexual themes, mentioned so far, do not speak of a "phallic cult" as this concept is usually understood. For example, in representations of anthropomorphous vases with genitals, the size of the virile organ is directly related to the use of the containers as drinking vessels the liquid being taken through the penis orifice; on the other hand both phalluses and vulva are shown... Nor is a phallic purpose the main function of all genital representations (the toasters); that is, they are not genital representations that of themselves constitute a cult. Thus a simple naked figure cannot be classified as an object of a "phallic cult".

There are, however, archaeological objects that do seem to suggest that in ancient Peru also there was a type of the universally known "phallic cult", that is the exaltation of the male sex organ as a symbol of virility and fecundity. The examples that best testify to such a "phallic cult" in Peru, are comprised by stone sculptures that adopt the shape of a penis, shown in a larger size [Fig. 109].

The uyo (= penis) here referred to as a possible example of a version of a "phallic cult" are stone

Fig. 107. Man with a phallic hair style. The phallus seems to represent virility, and not the exaltation of the penis which characterizes the "phallic cult" (Vicús, R. M. Pereyra Collection).

Fig. 108. Tripod standing on three phalluses, and which likewise is not a piece representative of a "phallic cult" (Vicús, R. Larco Herrera Museum).

Fig. 109. Stone phallus or uyo of stylized form. (Sillustani, Puno).

sculptures that show an erect male sexual organ with the gland, free of the prepuce, stylistically depicted. In one of these stone uyos in the Larco Herrera Museum (Larco, 1966: 10) the gland adopts the shape of a human head; it seems, judging by the stylistic features present in this stone, that it comes from the region of Pallasca. There are other examples of stone uyos in the National Museum of Anthropology and Archaeology (Lima) of unknown age and provenance. But uyos abound —in the light of present knowledge— specially on the high tableland in the region of Titicaca and we offer some details about these:

---

(1) We should not confuse them with the early Vicús and Moche warriors, the cut of whose hair imitates the penis gland; these expressions have already been commented upon and it has been concluded that they do not represent phalluses, but are phallic symbols worn by personages and translated into allusions to strength and virility. S. Lafone Quevedo (1950) supposed that even the maces and the helmets of the Moche warriors had a phallic implication which cannot be disregarded outright except that here we are faced with a situation similar to that of the "phallic hairdress" already mentioned, which seem to symbolize virility or strength on a plane where the idea of fecundity does not enter, as it would if this were a concept of "phallic cult".

In 1971-72, the author had the opportunity of examining an important group of these uyos, sculptured in stone, coming undoubtedly, from Chucuito (Puno), though they had been removed from their original site (KD, 1976: 148-49). Some, perhaps the most important of them today adorn the patio of an old mansion in Chucuito (1). Other specimens belonging to the series, found by the people of that area in the course of their farm labors, and also during the archaeological cleaning of the monument called Inca-uyo, located in the plaza of Chucuito,

77

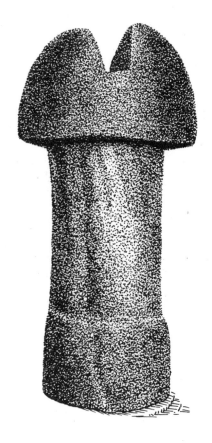

Fig. 110. Stone phallus (Sillustani, Puno).

and occasionally the penis meatus, is emphazised by a deep line [Fig. 107]. Evidently, the uyos must have been planted in the ground, since they have a sort of stem or platform, elongated, square or cylindrical, which was stuck in the ground and due to its weight firmly held the phallus vertical in the ground. It is impossible to know if the places where they were situated were specially chosen; but the abundance of these objects in places coming from neighbouring sites near Chucuito, allow us to infer that, perhaps, they were placed within the boundaries of farms or fields. They probably served as objects for attracting, through magic, an abundance of crops and cattle. From the large size of the archetype of the stone uyos from Chucuito it is evident that they were not objects used in deflowering practices.

started specially by Ruiz Estrada when the author was in charge of the general technical direction of studies in the region of Puno, have been carried away and put in the small yard of a house in Chucuito (1). The uyos referred to are of different sizes, some worked more simply than others [Fig. 106]. In these stone phalluses, the gland,

(1) Ruiz Estrada collected, with extreme care, an important number of these stone phalluses which he put in a temporary place, "planting" them in a small adjacent yard. This has led to conjectures rashly expressed regarding the existence of a "phallic garden" in Chucuito, without explaining that the place they occupy and the noticeable crowding of the pieces are fortuitous and of recent date.

78

Figs. 111-112. Life and death are a cicle. This is the only way to explain the presence of towers like the ones of Sillustani, Mollocahua (bottom) and others, shaped like large phalluses. These towers served as funerary dwellings.

22. Phallus-shaped Funerary Towers: the Chullpa

Superficial explorations of funerary towers or "chullpa" carried out in Sillustani and other archaeological sites of Puno by the author in 1971-72 and specially in 1974, have led him to sustain the hypothesis that those funerary towers, rising to 12 meters in height are like a phallus in shape [Figs. 111, 112]. There are multiple reasons for this which have been extensively treated (KD, 1976: 270-72). The two principal ones being the general shape of the chullpa, and the ring that surrounds the upper part of it which seems to correspond to a stylistic allusion to a gland freed from the prepuce. The formal variations of the "chulpa" do not destroy the hypothesis; most of them seem to reinforce it. If this is true, we are here faced by a new modality that could be considered as a "phallic cult" which is "not necessarily equivalent to eroticism: it falls within a magic-propitiatory context for the multiplication and abundance of vegetables and animals for food" (KD, 1976: 272).

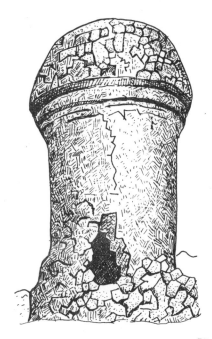

23. Representation of Sexual Diseases?

References abound in the chronicles of the XVI and XVII Centuries to general diseases, and particularly those related to sex.

On the other hand, representation of diseases, specifically of venereal diseases, are scarce or very difficult to classify with precision as such because of the vagueness with which pathological conditions are portrayed in pottery.

Such is the case of the destructive lesions observed in the faces of some ceramics, which are probably due to punishment mutilations, and not necessarily to scars left by certain diseases, such as syphilis for example (Lastres, 1943). In addition faces partly eaten away present in sculptural pottery, including Moche, should not necessarily be considered affected by syphilic lesions. Nevertheless studies of syphilis in ancient Peru can draw on another source used by Tello (1909) and Tello and Williams (1930): skulls and long bones, gathered in old cemeteries, which, according to the scholars mentioned, show lesions due to pathological processes. Discussion on this theme of the antiquity of syphilis in Peru, however, still continues.

There are some Moche representations of persons shown suffering from some disease. Even though it is impossible today to determine if the origin of those diseases was venereal, it is interesting to note that the ceramist intended to insinuate, in certain cases, a relationship between the disease and sex. Two pieces of that kind were examined by the author, one in a public museum, the other

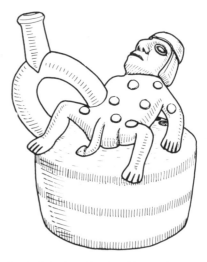

Fig. 113. Patient showing skin eruptions, perhaps related to sex (Moche, N.M.A.A., Lima).

Fig. 114. Person manipulating his genitals; he tries, apparently, to eliminate a tumour that bothers him (Moche, N.M.A.A., Lima).

80

Fig. 115. Subject lying down, suffering from a skin disease. The author does not think that this type of representation alludes necessarily to homosexuals, as has been said. Nor does he consider that the aim of the ceramist-sculptor would necessarily have been to show that the disease had a connection with sex (Moche, A. Fehling Museum, Lima).

in a private one [Figs. 113, 115]. In the Rafael Larco Herrera Museum there are specimens similar to one of the above mentioned pieces [Fig. 115]: a man (with a mask of Aiapaec?), naked from the waist down, is lying showing his genitals. To do this he holds one of his legs with his hand, if indeed he is not rubbing it, according to a more reasonable interpretation. This pottery scene is popularly considered as a probable representation of a homosexual lying in such a posture that he shows his buttocks and flaccid genitals. The expression of despair on his face and the little plate at his feet, perhaps containing curative substances (1), suggest the possibility that the personage may be a patient suffering from a skin disease, not necessarily connected with sex (2), who is busy rubbing his body with some medicament.

The other pottery piece, from the National Museum of Anthropology, is even more illustrative than the one mentioned above, though both belong to the same thematic sphere [Fig. 113]. Specimens of similar scenes exist, which are considered to be representations of sexual impotence, due to the fact that the naked individual, shows phallic flaccidity. But the very fact that the Moche ceramist represented a sick man must have led him to show the patient with a flaccid penis; that undoubtedly, is not the same as necessarily identifying this representation as sexual impotence... There is no doubt that the subject shown is suffering from a disease: the circles scattered all over his body must refer to

(1) In other examples relating to the same theme (Tello, 1938: 67), the patient is shown taking medicines or searching for relief through rubbing from the stinging sensation produced by the disease.

(2) Naturally this supposition does not disregard others such as that the disease represented, not necessarily sexual, was the reason for sexual lack of interest or inactivity.

stylizations of eruptions present on his skin (1). Even though there are no weighty reasons for maintaining that the iconographic scene we are studying refers to a sexually impotent man, the legs spread to reveal in an obvious way a flaccid penis, lead to the suspicion that the disease suffered from was linked to sex (2).

---

(1) There are other representations of this specimen, where it seems evident that the detail of the plate filled with a granulated substance refers to the medicament which the patient seems to be rubbing on his skin.

(2) We must bear in mind that a desperate patient no longer has an erect penis.

24. Punishment for Sexual Crimes

About sexual crimes and their punishment, the only information is that detailed in the chronicles of the XVI and XVII Centuries. Guaman Poma illustrates his works, with drawings of people punished for infringement of sexual laws, specially of adultery [Figs. 119, 120].

Moche pottery representations show us the infliction of punishments such as hurling a convict over a cliff, mutilating lips and nose [Fig. 117], amputating arms and legs, exposing persons —naked and lashed to a post— and leaving them as victims of

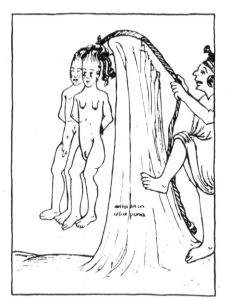
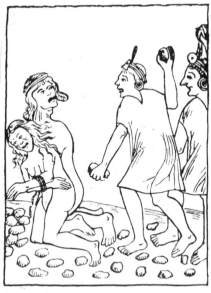

The historical iconography of Guaman Poma offers drawings related to punishments for sexual crimes. With relation to these, Guaman Poma gives some details, and even quotes mournful verses repeated by prisoners. Fig. 119. Two subjects punished for fornication (huachoc) —pre marital copulation— are hanged by their hair from the aranay, or stone, turned into a gallows. Fig. 120. Adulterers are stoned "in the place called uinpillay"; if it was found that one of the parties was less guilty, he received a whipping.

116

117

Among the representation of people undergoing punishment some must refer to chastisements because sexual rules had been violated, specifically those that protect the unity of the family. Fig. 118. Of the three drawings here shown, only this seems to refer to a punishment related to sex (R. Larco Herrera Museum, Lima). Fig. 116. A person tied to a post being devoured by birds of prey (E. Seler). Fig. 117. Person that has been mutilated, perhaps not for misdeeds of a sexual nature, but to drain off his blood in order to offer it in sacrifice, as is evident in other iconographic examples where such acts are portrayed (KD, 1966; 1969: fig. 425. See also Kutscher, 1954).

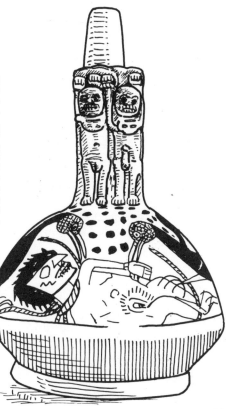

118

birds of prey [Fig. 116]... Nevertheless it is impossible to isolate cases which refer to acts of punishment applied specifically to those who broke the rules in matters of sex, except, perhaps, the representation of a man and a woman tied together and waiting to be devoured by birds [Fig. 118]... Nor is it possible to draw inferences about the rules governing sexual matters other than that there must have been some precepts in the home sphere to protect the integrity of the family; a matter which concerned the State in the ancient high cultures of America (Trimborn, 1968). In fact, the punishment for breaking laws of sexual behaviour must have been applied in cases of adultery for instance, rather than to punish certain sexual forms such as oral or anal coitus. According to known archaeological representations, those practices were not necessarily repudiated or prohibited; nevertheless, they must have existed together with a group of restrictive rules...

25. *Sexuality Among Animals*

Moche pottery offers a repertory of sexual scenes where the protagonists are animals [Figs. 121-127]. These representations must be considered separately from those showing human beings with animal heads, of a magic nature. Thus, we also exclude from the group the case of probable scenes of

zooerasty. Finally representations of mythical zooerasty are likewise omitted from this chapter.

Gebhard (1973: 9: 29) has gathered synthesized information on the theme: "majority of the scenes (over 90%) are coital and the animals generally are mammals; most of them are quadrupeds which I have not been able to identify; they might be deer, llamas, vicuñas or other similar ungulates. Some of the most vague, the most generalized, are dogs. Regarding coital representations, some 27% of the animals are identifiable quadrupeds: 13% are llamas; 16% rats or mice; 19%, frogs or toads; and 19% are mythological creatures. The census is completed by a pair of jaguars, another of crustaceans, and a mixed pair. The postures adopted are generally proper to the species; but in some cases, coitus is accomplished in the human way, with one animal supine and the other one on top of it. Except for a case of self-fellatio, there are no fellatory representations; masturbation is quite rare [Fig. 125], and genital exhibition uncommon".

Finally we can question the aims of the ceramist when representing scenes of animal sexual behaviour. Except for figures of beings involved, apparently, in a lax mythological or rather fabled sphere, corresponding to animals of indeterminate shape, shown copulating, the iconography we refer to does not seem to be inspired by anything other than naturalistic repetition, in clay, of zoological sexuality, as conceived by the ceramist. We find no reasons which support the supposition that it might have been "didactical material", because

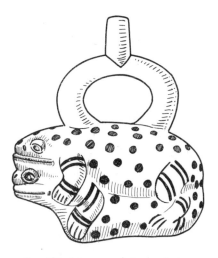

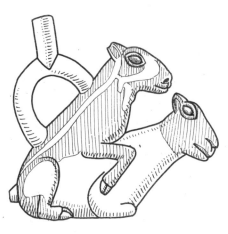

Fig. 121. Intercourse between batrachians (Moche, N.M.A.A. — Nº 1/4195).

Fig. 122. Intercourse between llamas (Moche, N.M.A.A. — Nº 39980).

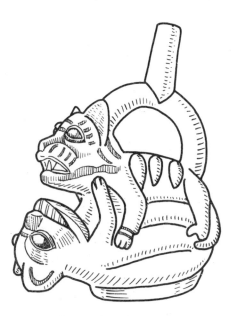

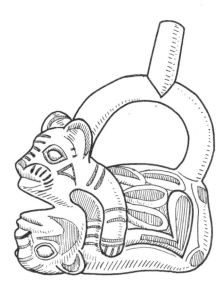

Fig. 123. Animals, perhaps felines, during intercourse (Moche, N.M.A.A. Nº 408/10).

Fig. 124. Animals imitating human copulation (Moche, N.M.A.A. — Nº 1/4185).

85

125

Animal sexuality: Fig. 125. Dog masturbating itself, in a way similar to human beings. (Art Museum). Fig. 126. Mice copulating (Moche, N.M.A.A. — Nº 1/4193). Fig. 127. A basically animal mythological being, wearing a cap, copulates with a batrachian (Moche, N.M.A.A. Nº 1/4218).

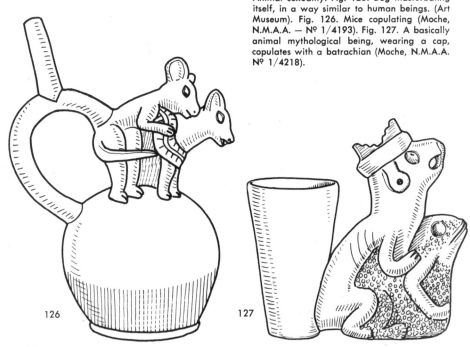

126

127

these representations appear in a medium where man had deep and daily contact with nature in all its magnitude... It may be possible in certain specimens to trace a breath of humour, inspired perhaps by some amusing fable; this is suggested by the three toads in simultaneous intercourse, or the pair of mice copulating while the male mouse grasps a peanut shell [Fig. 126].

FINAL NOTE: A summary containing general conclusions is given in the introduction of the book. Conclusions on the different topics discussed (fellatio, homosexuality, etc.) are included in each chapter of this work. For these reasons it is unnecessary in the present case to offer a final summary.

ADDITIONAL INFORMATION ABOUT SEXUALITY IN ANCIENT PERU (*)

(*) Glossary of words in Alphabetical order related to sexuality, extracted particularly from the chronicles of the XVI and XVII Centuries. Therefore, this information refers to the last years of the Inca Empire. Some words even refer to habits still surviving in Peru.

ABORTIVES

There are references in the chronicles to certain plants used as abortives, for instance the Huachana (Euphorbia huachanchana). To avoid abortion, the huacata (Togetes Minuta) was used.

ABSTINENCE

Sexual abstinence was practised in cases demanded in ceremonies or worship. The chroniclers refer to it by the word "fasting".

ACATAYMITA

Festival celebrated "to ripen the fruit" in December, when "the avocados start to ripen". It lasted for six days and nights: "men and boys completely naked, gathered in a small square among the orchards, and ran from there to a distant hill, and they had access to whatever woman they caught in the race". In the "Relation of the Augustines" there is a brief reference that seems to be connected to the Acataymita. Tello identified the scene of the Acataymita in pre-Inca Moche pottery.

ACLLA

Young women, chosen for their beauty, who lived closely guarded in the acllahuasi. A group of them was dedicated to religious worship. The rest of them spun, wove and prepared a beverage made of fermented corn (chicha); the Inca used them as concubines, and particularly to present as gifts to distinguished people. (see: COITUS: MASSIVE AND PUBLIC).

ACLLAHUASI

House where the acllas lived. (See: ACLLA; EUNUCHS).

ADULTERY

Sexual extra-marital contact was punished in the Inca Empire, sometimes even with death. (See: POLIGAMY PUNISHMENT).

AMOROUS CARESSES

There are few archaeological representations on the sexual theme where amorous caresses are found. These must not be confused with manipulation, fellatio or masturbation.

ANIMATED CORPSES
(See: CARCANCHA).

APHRODISIACS
(See: HUANARPO; MASSAU).

BESTIALITY
The natives of the Peruvian highlands are, even today, reputed to perform sexual acts with llamas. Though there might be isolated cases, this practice does not seem as common as supposed. Pachacuti may be referring to this practice when he says: "...which they commited with animals..." for which the Incas punished them. Pottery with representations on that subject was apparently broken deliberately in the XX Century...

CAHUILLACO
Female mythological personage, who, after waking up, eats a lucuma fruit, which before falling from the tree, had been fertilized by the deity Cuniraya, transformed into a little bird.

CAPULLANA
Female government, or gynecocracy, was centered in a matron or "capullana"; this practice still survived isolatedly on the North Coast of Peru when the Spaniards arrived. The Capullana was also given the name of Tallapona.

CAPYAMA
Female mythological personage who was made pregnant by Cullquiri transformed into a bird ("callacallo"); captured by Capyama, he "joined her and grew in the woman's womb", and she gave birth to Cullquiri himself, transformed into a "beautiful young man".
(See: CULLQUIRI).

CARCANCHA
Skeleton, or, better, "animated corpse". Word applied by KD to define the skeletonised being in action, represented in pottery.

CONTRACEPTIVES
Perhaps the coitus per-anum was a way of avoiding pregnancy; there is much archaeological evidence.

CASTRATION
(See: EUNUCHS).

COCA
H. Valdizán saw in the "cocaine psychosis" the origin of the archaeological representations on the sexual theme and he therefore assumed that it affected the "location of the libido". But the use of coca (Erythroxyon coca) was not limited to Moche culture...

COITUS
(See: Yoccu).

COITUS WITH BIRDS
(See: GUACAMAYA; CAPYAMA; CUNIRAYA).

COITUS (MASSIVE AND PUBLIC)
The chronicler Pachacuti states that Huascar ordered all the acllas or chosen women to be gathered in the plaza, and ordered one hundred dancers to copulate with them in public in order to impress a group of curacas of high hierarchy.

COITUS (MYTHICAL)
See: RUCANACUTU; CHAUPIÑANCA; HUATYACURI URPIHUACHACA; GUACAMAYA; CUNIRAYA, etc.).

CUCHIMILCO
Small clay or terra-cotta figure, generally female, in which sexual characters are barely noted. The Chancay "cuchimilcos" are famous. They may be related to the fertility cult. (See: PACHAMAMA).

CULLQUIRI
Mythological personage who desired the beautiful Capyama, and won her by means of a pact: Cullquiri must previously open an irrigation canal. (See: CAPYAMA).

CUNIRAYA
(See: CAHUILLACO; URPIHUACHACA).

CUNTURCUTU
Place to which Huatyacuri went in order to marry the daughter of Tamtañanca, according to mythological legends. (See: HUATYACURI).

CHAMICO
Solanaceae plant used for preparing a toxic beverage. It is commonly said, referring to a man under the domination of a woman, that he has "been given chamico" (Datura ferox).

CHAUPIÑANCA

Elder sister of Urpihuachaca, according to Huarochiri myths, who, in some legends, as the wife of Huatyacuri. In ancient times "when he wore a human shape and form, he prostituted himself (copulated) with all the Huaccas..." (See: URPHIHUACHA-CA and RUCANUCUTU).

CHIARIAJE

Ritual battles between neigbouring groups, still taking place periodically in Cuzco. These are fights to the death, with simple ancient weapons; death during combat propitiates the fertility of the soil... The prizes are the young women spectators of the battle who sing meanwhile, and to whom the victors are joined in servinacuy.

CHUQUISUSU

Female mythological personage, who does not succumb to the amorous intentions of the deity Pariacaca before demanding from him previously, as a compensation, the opening of an irrigation channel.

ENGAGEMENT

See: TINCUNACUSPA).

EUNUCHS

The chronicles inform us of the presence of eunuchs or castrated men, as guardians in the acllahuasi. There are archaeological representations of subjects practising self-castration.

FEMPELLEC

Mythological personage who governed the Lambayeque valley. "The Demon appeared before him in the shape and form of a beautiful women (...). Fempellec slept with her and after such infamous intercourse, it started raining (...), and this deluge lasted for thirty days...". Other calamities followed, so Fempellec was bound and thrown into the sea.

GUACAMAYA

Myth according to which two brothers who survive the Flood are served with food and drink by two "bird-women" (Guacamayas) who try to remain undiscovered. Surprised by one of the brothers, a Guacamaya escapes by flying away while the other is seized. The myth ends by saying that from this union mankind descended.

GUACANQUI

(See: SEDUCTION).

GUAYANAY

(See: ILLA).

GYNECOCRACY

(See: CAPULLANA).

HAPIÑUÑO

According to González Holguín, this was a "phantom or dwarf" who used to appear with two long breasts..." There are other ancient allusions to the hapiñuño.

HERMAPHRODITES

There is only one pottery specimen, Virú, representing an authentic hermaphrodite. Ancient supplications to the deity, in quechua, perhaps do not say that this was hermaphrodite, but asexual as archaeological iconography seems to suggest. Hermaphrodites are cited by Pachacuti (XVI C.).

HOMOSEXUALITY

Forbidden and repudiated by the Incas. Cieza (1553) gives information about sexuality among the people of Huayla, and tells us also about a type of religious homosexuality. In the archaeological material that has survived until our days, there are only two specimens: Vicús and Moche. Pachacuti refers to homosexuals as "sodomites". (See: HUAYLAYO; SODOMY).

HOMOSEXUALITY (MYTHOLOGICAL)

(See: OTOYA).

HOMOSEXUALS FOR THE TROOPS

The chronicler Pachacuti refers to the fact that (in Tupac Yupanqui's days). "many young men were raised who were not to know women; these afterwards served the warriors in battle". The reference is, nevertheless, somewhat confused.

HUANARPO

Aphrodisiac of vegetable origin. Two varieties were used ("female" and "male"); the china-huanarpo (Jatropha basiacantha, Pax and K. Hoffman) and the orco-huanarpo (Jatropha macrannantha, Mull, Arg). (See: MASSAU).

HUARACHICO

Transition rite when the young man reached puberty. In women, this was called quicochico.

HUARMIMUNACHI

Amulets which assured that the owner's love would be requited (Valdizán).

HUATYACURI

Mythological male personage, considered as son of the god Pariacaca, who cures the powerful Tantañanca by finding the cause of his disease: While his wife toasted corn, "a grain jumped into her parts, which gave food (to a man), and from that moment her relations were illicit..." As his price before curing Tantañanca, he demanded to sleep with his daughter: she did not accept until she saw her father cured.
(See: CUNTURCUTU).

HUAYLAYO

Quechua word, found by KD in the ancient region of Conchucos. It is equivalent to something like effeminate, because of the tasks performed, and, by extension, a homosexual. It is interesting to notice that the phrase: "May the Guaylas go after you" was found by Cieza when referring to homosexuals in ancient Peru, since there seems to be a linguistic relation between "Guaylas" and "Huaylayo".
(See: HOMOSEXUALITY).

ICHICOLLCO

Popular legendary personage (Ancash-Huánuco): small, bearded, sensuous, living near fountains or in solitary places who rapes the young women who walk there.

ILLA (or LLIRA)

In mythology, wife of Quitumbe and mother of Guayanay. When her husband did not return, Illa demanded vengeance from the god Pachacamac and the Sun, who listened to her and sent "a great storm..." In gratitude, Illa tried to sacrifice her own son, but he was saved by a "Royal Eagle".

ILLA (MAJOR)

Sculptural amulet in "Huamanga Stone", used, even today, in agriculture. It represents a farming estate, and a row of bulls. There are "Illas" in other shapes and designs.

INCEST

Incestuous marriage was not tolerated, except in the case of dynastic incest practised in the ruling caste of the Incas, which took place between brothers and sisters.

KISS

Oral contact was known, judging by archaeological iconography; there are no representations of total kisses.
(See: PACHACAMAC).

LESBIANISM

There are no references to lesbianism in the chronicles, nor in archaeological material.

LINEAGE

Both noble and common women behaved according to specific rules, as stated by Garcilaso. On the other hand, noble women could only marry nobles.
(See: OLLANTA).

MAGIC PREGNANCY

Even today, there are native girls who say they have been made pregnant by lightning or the rainbow. (Field Reports, KD, 1956).
(See: ICHICOLLCO).

MANCHAYPUITO

A legend, from the colonial or republican period, which tells of the love between a native woman with a Spanish or half-breed priest. When his beloved dies the priest makes a quena from one of her long bones and composes a sad melody known as the "manchaypuito". There are those who think that this legend has its origin in Incaic Peru.

MASSAU (MASHUA)

The MASSAU was an aphrodisiac (Tropaelum tuberosum), which, as Cobo notes, was given to soldiers so that they would not feel any sexual urges. Cobo's massau is the mashua.

MOCHE

Coastal culture (IV-VIII Centuries A.D.) from which proceeds most of the information in pottery regarding pre-hispanic sexuality. It is followed by the Vicús Culture, also coastal, and Virú; both of them are earlier than Moche but related to it.

MONOGAMY

People had to practice monogamy. They were forbidden, under threat of punshment and even death, to have several wives.
(See: POLIGAMY).

NAKED DANCES

In mythology, these were performed in honor of the female deity Chaupiñanca. The dancers were men, who finished by dancing "completely naked, as they thought that Chaupiñanca seeing them that way" would get greater enjoyment.
(See: ACATAYMITA).

NAKEDNESS

It is necessary to distinguish between simple nakedness: of prisioners being made to walk in procession or naked bodies for sacrifice (Sechín, Moche, Chancay), and nakedness in a sexual context.

(See: ACATAYMITA).

ÑUSTA

Quechua name given to young women of the nobility. When they married, they were called pallas. The legal wife of the Inca was the coya.

OLLANTA

Also Ollantay. Name of a theater piece of colonial times with an incaic theme and perhaps based on a pre-hispanic poem. General Ollantay desires Cusicollor, the daughter of the Inca, but his condition of common citizen does not allow him to marry her. He therefore rebels but is defeated. Finally the Inca, in a paternal gesture makes an exception and gives him Cusicollor.

OTOYA

Youngest son of Tumbe, who, according to mythology was given to "sensuality and drinking". In his time, some "giants came to the earth". As these "had no women and practised the infamous sin" (homosexuality), they were punished by God, who sent them "a rain of fire flakes...". This myth survives in Chacña and has been analyzed together with other versions (KD, 1978: 45).

PACCHA

Containers used in the fertility cult. KD calls "sexual paccha" the ones having the shape of genitals.

PACHAMAMA

"Mother Earth", to which in ancient Peru a cult was dedicated. Perhaps the small figures or cuchimilcos are a symbol of it.

PACHAMANCA

Word, still in force, which means "pot (or plate) cooked in the ground". By extension, "pachamanca" is a group of heterogeneous articles, and also caressing accompanied generally by manipulation.

PAMPAHUARMI

Quechua word for prostitute. The pampahuarmis are mentioned by D. de Santo Tomás (1560), González Holguín (1608),

Garcilaso (1609) and others. Though the quechua word for whore exists, prostitution in the Inca Empire has yet to be studied, as W. Espinoza (1972) rightly says when he raises a series of questions on the subject. What Ramos Gavilán says about the building ordered to be erected in Copacabana for beautiful women dedicated to sexual activity with the mitmaes, is not equivalent to the classical concept of prostitution, as in any case this activity would have produced no special recompense to the pampahuarmis or mitahuarmis. Perhaps it might be understood as a synonym of acllahuasi; or a "popular" type of this made up of women in mita (turns) appointed to give sexual satisfaction. The lack of further information does not permit additional inferences to be drawn. There is a study by M.A. Denegri (1977) on prostitution in ancient Peru.

PAMPERA

In Lima, slang word applied to women of free and easy virtue who are not prostitutes. It is interesting to note that the word seems to be a hispanisation of the quechua term pampahuarmi, which does mean prostitute. (KD, 1969: 505).

PANTANACO

Name given to the Tincunacuspa, in the Relation of the Augustines.

PARIACACA

(See: CHUQUISUSU).

PATHOLOGY

Certain authors saw in Moche pottery representations of sexual theme an answer to patholoical conditions.

(See: COCA; SKULL MALFORMATIONS).

PHALLIC CULT

According to the studies carried out by the author, the uyos and the "phallic towers" of Sillustani, etc., may be evidence of a phallic cult.

PHALLIC CULT (MALE)

In mythology, "the men who had a short organ" offered worship "to the vigorous Rucanacutu" begging him "to make it longer".

PERNADA

"Right" of the "godfather" to possess the bride sexually. This was a colonial habit which today is perhaps extinct.

PERVERSIONS
(See: SEXUAL THEME).

POLIGAMY
It was only permitted by the highest nobility (Inca) and the Inca and provincial nobility.
(See: MONOGAMY).

PORNOGRAPHY
(See: SEXUAL THEME).

PROSTITUTION
(See: PAMPAHUARMI; PAMPERA).

PROSTITUTION (MYTHICAL)
A way of "compensation" rather than of prostitution by agreeing to copulate for a material reward of social interest; we find it in the mythological legend of Chuquisusu.
See: CHUQUISUSU; CULLQUIRI).

PUNISHMENT
Thome, in mythology, brother of Guayamal, accused one of his sons of adultery and condemned him "to death by being torn in pieces".

QUITUMBE
(See: ILLA).

RABONA
In the last Century and even today a woman who followed her husband, by servinacuy or by marriage, on military campaigns. The soldier enjoyed the company of his wife and benefitted from her services as cook and carrier of part of his equipment.

RACA
Vulva, vagina. (Quechua word).

RUCANA
Quechua word for finger, and, in extension, phallus. Thus, Rucanacutu would mean: "large finger"; that is to say, "large phallus".
(See: RUCANACUTU).

RUCANACUTU
Name of a mythological personage who "fulfilled the desires of Chaupiñanca, to such an extent that Ch. considered him the best of all the Huaccas".
(See: CHAUPIÑANCA).

SEDUCTION WITH GUACANQUI
A "lamamichi" or shepherd was accepted by a young girl (accla,) though he was in rags. Being taken prisoner, the shepherd was found to have a "guacanqui" or love amulet; it was this that may have popularised the use of guacanquis.
(See: LINEAGE).

SEDUCTION (MYTHOLOGICAL)
In mythology, not only the man seduces and uses charms. (See: COITUS WITH BIRDS). Thus, a sister of Chuquisusu waits for Cullquiri in the road, "to seduce him, showing him her breasts and genitals" and inviting him to drink "chicha and ticti".

SENSUALITY
(See: OTOYA, FEMPELLEC).

SERVINACUY
(See: TINCUNACUSPA).

SEXUAL THEME
The concept of "sexual theme" is used by KD to refer to archaeological representations in which sexual figures or acts appear. This concept avoids the use of words such as "pornography", "degeneration", "pervertion", etc. denoting preconceived ideas.

SEXUAL HABITS
Sexual habits of Peruvian "natives" of today have been fundamentally described by M. Villavicencio.
((See: Bibliography).

SEXUAL ORGIES
The chroniclers, refer to collective orgies, tolerated on some occasions by the Inca rulers; on these occasions there was drinking, and sexual behaviour was lax among those present though it was not then considered a major offense nor was it punished.

SODOMY
The chroniclers refer to "sodomy" in a vague way, as they do not state whether anal coitus was also practised on the heterosexual plane. Heterosexual sodomy appears in many archaeological representations on the sexual theme (Moche).
(See: HOMOSEXUALITY).

SONCOAPA-CHINACOC
Also Huaca-chinacoc; amulets shaped like "very round small stones" with aphrodisiac powers, mentioned by Pachacuti.

93

SKULL DEFORMATIONS

A. Posnanski considered that Moche sexual pottery was related to the practice of deforming the skull. But skull deformation is not restricted to Moche culture...

SYPHILIS

Based on the remains of bones, Tello and Williams considered that syphilis existed in ancient Peru. Virchow and others do not accept this conclusion. Chroniclers wrote about the "bubos" present in some descendants of the Inca nobility in the days of the Spaniards; probably skin eruptions of the third phase of syphilis.

TAMTAÑANCA
(See: HUATYACURI).

TALLAPONA
(See: CAPULLANA).

THOME
(See: PUNISHMENT).

TINCUNACUSPA

Pre-hispanic custom which survives even today among Peruvian peasants under the hispanicised name of servinacuy, which consists of a sort of engagement with sexual relations which is accepted by the group It is a kind of first phase of marriage; and therefore gives rise to debates whether it should be classified as a "trial marriage".

URPIHUACHACCA

Mythological female personage, mother of two young girls, one of whom is put to sleep by the god Cuniraya, because "he wanted to lie with the other who was transformed into a dove and flew away".

UYO
Virile organ. Quechua word.
(See: PHALLIC CULT).

YOCCU

Copulation, in quechua, according to González Holguín. Yucunigui is the equivalent of "the man riding the woman", according to D. de Santo Tomás (1560).

COLOUR PLATES

* *A.A.N.M. or N.M.A.A.* = *Museo Nacional de Antropología y Arqueología, Lima. Art Museum* = *Museo de Arte, Lima.*

PLATE   III

Man with penis through which it was compulsory to drink fertilizing beverages. This would explain its extraordinary size in relation to the rest of the statue as well as the scant importance the sculptor gave to the representation of the testicles. Around the head twelve holes made it impossible to drink through that aperture. The man is seated and grasps the virile organ with one hand while with the other he maintains it erect. One of the few representations of the sexual theme emphasizing an apparently voluptuous and contented facial expression.

Moche. *White and red colors. A.A.N.M. 1/4294 Registration Number.*

PLATE IV

Feminine figure with a vulva to drink from. This belongs to a type of sexual "paccha". The exhibit need not necessarily be presented as a case of genital "showing", because its function was determined by the vulvar opening through which the magic liquid —probably with fertilizing properties— would flow directly to the mouth.

Moche. *Seated figure 18 centimeters high. Art Museum.*

PLATE   V

Anthropomorphous vessel showing the virile organ erect. This curious piece has no hole in the meatus sector and is therefore out of the usual run having no other function than that of simple exhibition. If it is authentic —as it appears to be— the lack of function is probably due to the fact that it was copied from older shapes which were indeed functional.

Moche *(?), Albert Fehling Museum.*

PLATE VII

Genitals separately represented. The generative member, though not totally erect, shows the uncovered penis. The liquid previously lodged in the testicles drains off through the meatus. For this reason it is possible to include this piece as a variant of the sexual "paccha", where in order to drink it was necessary to put the phallus directly in the mouth.

Moche. *Private collection.*

PLATE VIII

Human shape with phallus to drink from ("human paccha"). The penis is reduced to a glans of enormous proportions in comparison with the size of the figure. The gigantic size of the penis was not due to a "libidinous" intention but rather to the fact that the specific purpose of the vessel, when drunk from, was for the phallus to be placed in the mouth, probably in order to swallow fertilizing substances obtained through magic formulae. It is thus only to our eyes that the person appears really "humorous".
Recuoide *(Vicús?). Private collection.*

PLATE IX

A pair of phalluses take the place of the two spouts of a vessel.
Both have tiny holes and for that reason the author believes they represent a version of the penis, to oblige them to be brought to the mouth for drinking.
Vicús. *Red color with black geometrical negative paint. Albert Fehling Museum.*

PLATE X

*Amorous scene, with mouth contact. Perhaps in
this scene a tongue kiss has been represented
without necessarily introducing the tongue into the
woman's mouth. The male, an animated-corpse or
"carcancha" —with the head shown as a skull—
carries an "antara" or pipes of Pan and wears a
headdress ressembling a turban surmounted by a
little animal head. Both figures are dressed without
exposing or indicating their genitals. The man has
his arm round the woman's neck.*
Moche. *Light red color. A.A.N.M. 1/4370 Regis-*
tration Number.

PLATE XI

Coitus. Supine woman with her feet resting on the thighs of the male who is standing with flexed knees. The woman is resting on a matting but she is raising her body as if to reach the man's shoulder or even his face with her hands. It would seem that she was trying to tear away part of his headdress, or to cover his eyes, which she has partly done. Moche. *A.A.N.M. 1/4323 Registration Number.*

PLATE XII

Coitus. Woman in supine position with her arms and legs clutching the male's body. He bends down towards a prone position, legs flexed and feet resting on the floor. His lips are pressed tightly together and his look is vague, which would perhaps indicate that the potter-sculptor wanted to show an orgasm, making this a singular piece. At the same time it should be noted that the male is completely dressed during copulation. An examination of the back of the vessel shows that the male has loosened his trousers or huara *pulling them to one side to free his genitals of which only the testicles are indicated.*

Moche. *Red and white colors A.A.N.M. 1/9708 Registration Number.*

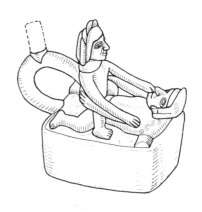

PLATE XIII

Coitus. The man is in a supine position with his legs separated and flexed, his head resting on a cylindrical pillow. The woman, with spread legs, is seated on the male genital region. Her vulva appears quite clearly, but not the anus to which no attention was paid in this case.

Moche. *Red and white colors with black geometrical ornaments. It is a vessel of high technological quality. A.A.N.M. Valle/10 Registration Number.*

PLATE   XIV

Coitus. The woman is in a supine posistion with her legs raised in the air. The man appears kneeling. Early Moche. White and red colors. Private collection.

PLATE XVI

*Coitus in a face-to-face seated position. The person-
ages are either tattooed or have painted bodies, or
they are dressed.*
Recuay. *Negative painting. A.A.N.M. 1/1353
Registration Number.*

PLATE XVII

Coitus. The woman is reclining on one side with her legs flexed. The male is also resting on one side penetrating her from behind while at the same time he has imprisoned the woman's legs with one of his own. The woman appears to be pregnant, judging from the bulkiness of her abdomen and breasts, one of which is held by her consort. The fact that she is pregnant is perhaps corroborated by the special position adopted for copulation.
Moche. *Two shades of red and white colors. A.A. N.M. 1/4367 Registration Number.*

PLATE XVIII

Anal coitus in the family bed. As the act takes place, the child beside the mother appears to be asleep. The contact is evidently per anum, *perhaps but not necessarily as a contraceptive measure. It should be noted that the vulva is shaped with the large lips closed. The penis, deeply penetrated, is scarcely seen.*

Moche. *White and red colors. 1/4317 Registration Number.*

PLATE XIX

Coitus, probably per anum, *takes place on a bed. The couple is covered with a blanket but the potter-sculptor has left the sexual parts and the legs exposed in order to achieve the purpose he had in mind. The little pillow is not used by the woman since she is slightly inclined to display her buttocks and thus facilitate the introduction of the penis.* Moche. *A.A.N.M. 1/4325 Registration Number.*

PLATE   XX

Coitus. The woman is in a supine position with flexed legs. The man, wearing a strange cap, appears to be kneeling behind her. It could be a heterosexual sodomite act but the faded representation does not permit a clear identification.
Chimú. (or "Tallan", from Tello). A vessel of two bodies joined by a stirrup-handle. A.A.N.M. 1/4262 Registration Number.

PLATE XXI

Coitus. Both persons naked performing the act on matting with a cylindrical pillow which the woman, crouching, holds with her arms and hands. The man seems to have an exceptionally thick phallus, not visible in the photograph. Both give the impression of a "mechanical" coitus. Perhaps we might say of this vessel that it is "didactic".

Moche. *White and red colors with incisions. A.A. N.M. 1/4369 Registration Number.*

PLATE XXII

Coitus. The woman appears in a prone position with her legs contracted and perhaps resting her belly on a sinuosity. The male holds her buttocks during the act.

Inca. *Coast tradition and provenance. From the collection of Mr. and Mrs. F.*

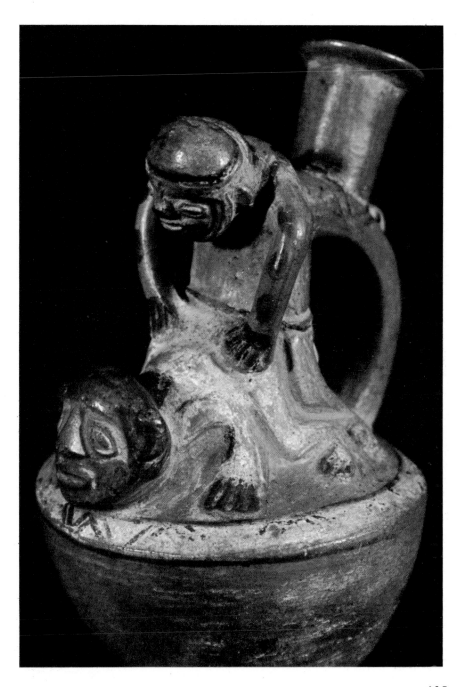

PLATE XXIII

Fellatio. The male is seated and the woman seems to be kneeling. The potter-sculptor did not perhaps exaggerate the size of the phallus —the fellatio woman keeping the prepuce folded back— as a "libidinous" exaggeration, but only to show clearly a fellatio scene.

Moche. *Private collection.*

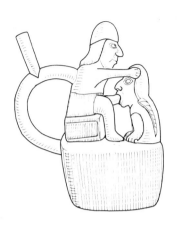

PLATE XXIV

Fellatio. The male is resting on a seat and holds the woman's head in his hands. Perhaps he is helping the fellatio-woman in her task.
Moche. *Red and white colors. This sculptured piece shows very high technological skill. A.A.N.M.*

PLATE XXV

Homosexual intercourse. The passive homosexual lies in a prone position with legs contracted. The active homosexual is also in a prone position, imprisoning the first with arms and hands. This is so far the only known case in Moche pottery showing homosexual intercourse. (In Vicús there is another one). The potter-sculptor shows the two men with naked buttocks and indicates very clearly the anus *penetration, while he also shows the flaccid penis of the passive homosexual in order to avoid any doubt.*

Moche. *Damaged piece. A.A.N.M.*

PLATE   XXVI

Sexual mating between animals. Representations of mythological or at least fabled characters. The female is apparently a toad; the male perhaps a bird (parrot?) wearing a strange headdress.
Chimú. *A dark, whistling vessel, which expels the whistle through holes placed in the head, and through others in the ears and mouth.*
A. 1/4218 Registration Number.

PLATE   XXVII

Sexual mating between animals. Mice. The male fastens his tail to the body of the female and holds there a peanut shell.
Late Moche. *Spherical vessel, white and red. A.A. N.M. 1/4193 Registration Number.*

PLATE XXVIII

Masturbation. Without being able to make a categorical assertion, this vessel seems to show a masturbator. The conclusion is based on the fact that similar versions exist (from the collection of shapes of husbands and wives) of persons with the same twisted facial expression who handle their phallus in an evident act of masturbation. The supposed onanist-masturbator has his penis erect and it stands out with the clarity of a "portrait". The thorax shows his ribs which would bring it close to the "carcancha" standard.

Early Moche *(perhaps from the Piura region). Mr. Seminario's former collection.*

PLATE   XXIX

*Masturbation. The person indulging in masturba-
tion is a "carcancha" as regards his head but this
is not necessarily to be interpreted as a moralizing
example since the "animated corpse" is presiding
over a greater "macabre" scene represented picto-
graphically round the body of the vessel.*
Moche. *The total height of the vessel is 21.5 cm.*
From The Art Museum.

PLATE   XXX

*Animal masturbation. This seems to be a dog in-
dulging in genital self-eroticism and adopting human
gestures. Indeed, while with one hand it grasps its
penis, with the other it covers its face as if it were
ashamed to be caught in the "lonely vice", very
much in the manner of the human onanist introduced by the author (see previous page).*
Midway Horizon. *Perhaps from Lambayeque. The
maximum height of the vessel is 17 centimeters.
From The Art Museum.*

PLATE   XXXI

"Carcancha" indulging in onanism. The skull-head and the lined ribs identify this personage as an animated-corpse or "carcancha". The visible penis together with the position of his hands allow the scene to be defined as an act of masturbation. It is not easy to draw concrete inferences about the presence of the child calmly resting on the shoulders of the "carcancha".

Moche. *Height 21.5 cm. From The Art Museum.*

PLATE XXXII

A "carcancha" masturbation. This deals with a couple, where the male is an animated-corpse or "carcancha". The skull-head and the lines symbolizing ribs show him to be dead; though in the rest of his body he is a living creature, with erect genitals, who seems to hold the scrotum while the woman is masturbating it. This is not merely a superficial caress as can be seen from the glans freed from the foreskin and the position of the woman's hand.

Moche. *White and red. A.A.N.M. 1/4363 Registration Number.*

PLATE   XXXIII

Coitus. Shown by stylized lines between naked figures. Perhaps this was meant to refer to some ritual race, related to the fertility cult.
Late Nazca *("Chanca"). Height 14.5 cm. Red, red-brown, black and white. Albert Fehling Museum.*

PLATE   XXXIV

Phallic shape for vaginal or anal penetration. This curious object was not a "comforter" since it has a pipe through which liquids could flow from the meatus. Neither was it necessarily a deflowering instrument. Perhaps it was used to give enemas, or perhaps, through the vaginal conduct, substances which were considered fertilizing. The crosspiece seems to indicate that the instrument was used to penetrate the vagina or anus.
Moche. *Total length 27 cm. The penis is 8 cm long with a maximum diameter of 3.5 cm. Albert Fehling Museum.*

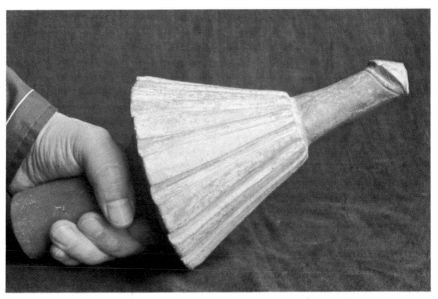

157

PLATE   XXXV

Person handling his own genitals (a self-operation, perhaps?). With one hand he stretches the scrotum forward so that the penis appears to one side; and with the other hand he holds something which appears to be a tumour he has removed from the scrotum.

Moche. *White paint on red. A.A.N.M. 1/4139 Registration Number.*

PLATE XXXVI

A reclining man showing circular skin lesions, perhaps the so-called buboes or gummas which appear during the tertiary period of syphilis. In any case it seems that the potter-sculptor wanted to explain that the illness had a sex relation. Note too the penis is presented as extremely flaccid.
Eearly Moche. *A.A.N.M. VF/10038 Registration Number.*

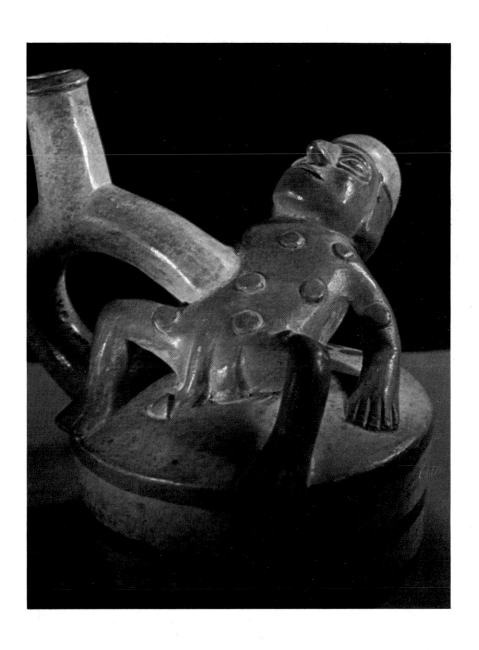

PLATE XXXVII

*A reclining man. A version of examples showing
persons attacked by some cutaneous disease which
produces itching, and which is cured by medicines
indicated here on a saucer. The exposition* ex pro-
feso *of the genitals would seem to mean that the
potter-sculptor wanted to point out that the pathological picture was related to some disease
contracted through sexual contact. We do not share
the popular idea that this is a warrior of rank with
homosexual tendencies who is displaying his buttocks. It is enough to look at the subject's afflicted
face in this and other examples in the series. It is
not possible to imagine that it is Aiapaec, the
divinity, who is suffering from the disease; perhaps
the person is only wearing his mask for magical
purposes.*
Moche. *White, red and black. Height 20.5 cm.
Albert Fehling Museum.*

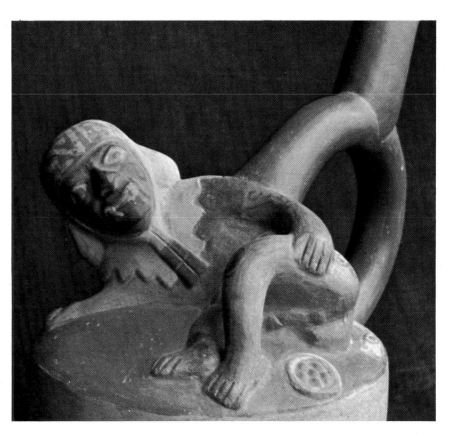

PLATE XXXVIII

Anthropophallus. The cap on the seated figure is shaped like a glans penis; the body is barely hinted at, likewise the outline of the penis, especially at the back of the vessel. The only opening is at the spout and the piece is formed by two conduits which are united.
Moche. *White and red. A.A.N.M. 1/4219 Registration Number.*

166

PLATE XL

Head with the nose transformed into genitals. Note the nose-phallus and the testicles, hinted at below the scrotum, which overhang the lips. Perhaps we can see also in the "earcap-ears" a phallic, testicular, metamorphosis. It is difficult to pronounce an opinion on the meaning which was given to this piece.

Moche *(Piura region?). From Mr. Seminario's former collection.*

PLATE XLI

Copulation, in series, by the divinity Ai-apaec. The woman is an earth creature and she is in a supine position; Aiapaec —or perhaps his deputy or masked chaman— is prone, kneeling over her. In the scene an assistant appears, in the form of a man-bird. Several figures can be seen round the vessel: cloistered women waiting their turn, watched over by a mythological being, and other characters whose duty apparently is to have food and drink ready.

Moche. *White, black and red colors. Height 21.5 cm. Albert Fehling Museum.*

172

BIBLIOGRAPHY(*)

BARRIONUEVO (A.)
1973   *Servinakuy*. Lima...

BASTO GIRON (L. J.)
1957   *Salud y enfermedad en el campe-
       sino peruano del siglo XVII*.
       Lima...

BERTONIO (L.)
1612   *Vocabulario de la lengua aymara*.

BRÜNING (H.)
       (Publicación aparecida en *An-
       thropophyteia*, v. 8; según Mue-
       lle, 1932).

CABIESES (F.)
1975   *Dioses y enfermedades* (...),
       v. 1. Lima...

CARRERA Y DAZA (F. de la)
1644   *Arte de la lengua Yunga*. Lima...

CARRION CACHOT (R.)
1923   "La mujer y el niño en el antiguo
       Perú" *Inca*. vol. 1: 32-354.
       Lima...
1955   "El culto al agua en al antiguo
       Perú". *Rev. Mus. Nac. Ant. Arq.*
       2, 2: 50-140. Lima...
1959   *La religión en el antiguo Perú*
       (...). Lima...

CIEZA DE LEON (P.)
1553   *Primera parte de la choronica
       del Perú* (...). Sevilla...

DENEGRI (M. A.)
1977a "Zooerastia: la llama, señorita de
       la altura". *Equis*, 84: 46-47.
       Lima... (Versión ampliada en
       MS, 1978).
1977b "La prostitución en al antiguo
       Perú". *Equis*, 85: 44-45; 86: 44.
       Lima...
1978   "Prostitución incaica". *Equis*,
       107, 108, 109. Lima...

FREZIER (A. F.)
1713   *Journal des Observations Physi-
       ques* (...) *de L'Amérique Meri-
       dionale*. París...

FRISANCHO PINEDA (D.)
1972   "Medicina popular e indígena".
       Acta Herediana, 4, 1: 18-24.
       Lima...

(*) Some ancient works, like those of
Pachacuti, are quoted in the text but do
not appear in this Bibliography in order not
to make it too extensive since they refer
to books of interest only to experts who
know where to locate these rare bibliogra-
phic items. All the works included in this
list have been consulted directly by the
author. General studies or those related to
the subject, like those of S. Freud, W.
Reich, H. Marcuse and others, have also
been personally examined but are not
included in order not to weaken the impact
of the contributions which deal more directly with the theme of this book.

GEBHARD (P. H.)
1970   "Sexual motifs in prehistoric
       Peruvian ceramics". T. BOWIE
       - C. V. CHRISTENSON, editors,
       Studies in Erotic Art. Basic
       Books, chapter 2. New York/
       London...
1973   "Motivos sexuales en la cerámica
       peruana prehistórica" *Fáscinum*,
       7: 10-30; 8: 9-37; 9: 9-34; 10:
       42-58. (Translated by M. A.
       DENEGRI). Lima...

GORBAK (C.) — LISCHETTI (M.) —
MUÑOZ (C. P.)
1962   "Batallas rituales del chiaraje y
       del tocto de la provincia de
       Kanas". *Rev. Mus. Nac.*, 31:
       245-304. Lima...

GUAMAN POMA DE AYALA (Ph.)
1936   *Nueva Coronica y Buen Gobierno
       de los Incas*. París...

GUTIERREZ NORIEGA (C.)
1938   "El pensamiento mágico en las
       pinturas del antiguo Perú". *Rev.
       Mus. Nac.* Lima...

JIMENEZ BORJA (A.)
1953   "La comida y los sentimientos
       sexuales". (*La comida en el an-
       tiguo Perú*, cap. en pp. 11-13).
       Lima...

JOYCE (Th. A.)
1923   "Pakcha". *Inca*, 1. Lima...

KAUFFMANN DOIG (F.)
1963a *El Perú arqueológico*. Lima...
1963b "Ñaymlap, ave totémica de los
       antiguos peruanos". (Publ. parcial

en *La Industria,* Chiclayo 1.1.
1964). Simposio de Arqueología...

1964 *La cultura Chimú* (Impresa en
163). Lima...

1966 *Mochica, Nazca, Recuay en la
arqueología peruana.* (Sobretiro
de *"La Universidad y el Pueblo".*
Segunda época, 4). Lima...

1969 *El Perú antiguo.* Hist. general de
los Peruanos, 1. (Publ. en sobretiro. Lima, 1970, con el título de
*Manual de Arqueología Perua-
na*). Lima...

1970 (Véase 1969).

1976 *El Perú arqueológico.* Lima...

1978 *Manual de arqueología peruana.*
(800 págs. — 1,500 figs.). Lima.

KINSEY (A. C.) and Others
1948 *Sexual Behavior, in Human Male.*
Philadelphia...

1953 *Sexual Behavior in Human Female.* Philadelphia...

KUTSCHER (G.)
1954 *Nordperuanische Keramik* (...).
"Monumenta Americana", 1.
Berlín...

LAFONE QUEVEDO (S.)
1950 "Ensayo mitológico. El culto a
Tonapa. Los himnos sagrados de
los reyes del Cuzco según el
Yamqui Pachacuti". *Tres relacio-
nes de antigüedades peruanas*
(Madrid, 1879). Ed. paraguaya,
pp. 285-353. Asunción...

LARCO HOYLE (R.)
1965 *La cerámica de Vicús.* 2 vs.
— (?) Lima...

1966 *Checán. Ensayo sobre las representaciones eróticas del Perú
precolombino.* Ginebra (Agosto).

1965 See: Larco, 1966.

LASTRES (J. B.)
1951 *Historia de la medicina peruana.*
(I: La medicina incaica). Lima

LASTRES (J. B.) — MUELLE (J. C.) —
FARFAN (J. M. B.) — GUILLEN (A.)
1943 *Representaciones patológicas en
la cerámica peruana.* Lima...

LIRA (J. A.)
1946 *Farmacopeca tradicional indígena
y prácticas rituales.* Lima...

LOTHROP (S. K.)
1955 "Peruvian Pacchas and Keros...".
Am. Antiquity, 31, 3.

LUMBRERAS (L. G.)
1978 *Pre-Inca erotic art.* Lima, Libre-
ría ABC... [The author's name
is not mentioned in this pam-
phlet, translated by Mr. Har-
rison]. Lima...

MARZAL (M. H.)
1977 "El servinakuy andino" (*Estudios
sobre religión campesina,* cap.
II). Lima...

MEJIA VALERA (J.)
1946 *Organización de la sociedad en
el Perú precolombino.* Lima...

MOLINA (Ch. — "el cusqueño")
s. XVI *Fábulas y ritos de los Incas*
(Lima, 1943). MS...

MUELLE (J. C.)
1932 "Lo táctil como carácter fundamental en la cerámica muchik.
Apuntes para una historia del
arte peruano". *Rev. Mus. Nac.,*
2, 1: 67-72. Lima...

PEREZ BARRADAS (J.)
1957 *Plantas mágicas americanas.*
Madrid...

PETERSEN (G.)
1955 "Adorno labial de oro usado por
los Tallanes". *Rev. Mus. Nac.
Ant. Arq.,* 2, 2: 161-168.
Lima...

POSNANSKY (A.)
1925 *Die erotischen Keramiken der
Mochicas und deren Beziehung zu
occipital deformierten Schädeln.*
(Abhandlungen zur Antropholo-
gie, Ethnologie und Urgeschichte,
2). Frankfurt...

1945 *Tihuanacu* (...). 4 vs. (2 ts.).
—57 New York y La Paz...

QUIJADA (O.)
Vida y sexo...

RAVINES (R.)
1974 "Amor indio. Crónica ilustrada
en barro". *Diners,* 26: 9-12.
Lima...

ROMERO (C. A.)
1923 "Tincunakùspa". *Inca,* 1: 83-91.
Lima...

176

TELLO (J. C.)
1909 *La antigüedad de la sífilis en el Perú.* Lima...
1938 *Arte antiguo peruano. Album fotográfico de las principales especies arqueológicas de cerámica Muchik existentes en los Museos de Lima* (Primera Parte. Tecnología y morfología). Inca, *vol. 2.* Lima...

TELLO (J. C.) — WILLIAMS (H. V.)
1930 "An ancient syphilitic skull from Paracas in Peru". *Ann. Med. History. Nouv. Serie,* 2 New York...

TERRAZOS CONTRERAS (M.)
1963a "Erotismo incaico". *Gente.* Lima (28 de Junio, pp. 40-42)...
1973b "El sexo en el antiguo Perú". *Ande y Mar,* 3: 6-7. Lima...

TRIMBORN (H.)
1935 "Der Ehebruch in den Hochkulturen Amerikas". *Anthropos,* 30: 533-547. Mödling...
1951 "Die Erotik in den Myten von Huarochirí". *Jahrbuch des Lindenmuseums.* (Neue Folge), 1. Stuttgart...
1968 *El delito en las altas culturas de América.* (Ed. alemana, 1938). Lima...

TSCHUDI (J. J. v.)
1918 *Contribuciones a la historia, civilización y lingüística del Perú antiguo.* (Col. Lib. Doc. Hist. Perú, 9 y 10). Lima...

URTEAGA-BALLON (O.)
1968 *Interpretación de la sexualidad en la cerámica del antiguo Perú.* Lima...

VALDIZAN (H.)
1915 *La alienación mental entre los primitivos peruanos.* Lima...

VELEZ LOPEZ (L.)
1912 *Las multilizaciones en los vasos antropomorfos del antiguo Perú.* Lima...

VILLAVICENCIO (V. L.)
1942 *La vida sexual del indígena peruano.* Lima...

WESTERMARCK (Ed. v.)
1902 *Geschichte der menschlichen Ehe,* Berlín...

WILLIAMS (H. V.)
1936 "Cross and microscopic anatomy of two Peruvian mummies". *Arch. Pathology Lab. Med. Chicago,* July)...

APENDIX

APHRODISIAC
Substance which produces excitement or sexual power. Anaphrodisiacs produce contrary effects.

ANTHROPOPHALLUS
Human figure representing a penis. Word coined by KD.

ANTHROPOVULVA
Human figure representing a camouflaged vulva. Word coined by KD.

ASEXUAL
Having no sex. Asexual representations frequently trace their origin to sexual taboos.

BESTIALITY
(See: ZOOERAST).

CARESSES
(See: MANIPULATION)

CASTRATION
The act of amputating the sex organ; self-castration if self-performed.
(See: EUNUCH).

CELIBACY
Sexual abstinence, specially with a religious motivation. It can be permanent or temporary Spanish chronicles referred to "fasting" as a temporary way of abstaining from sex and from certain food.

COITUS
Sexual relation; word applied not only to copulation, but also to anal and fellatio sexual relations.

COITUS (ANAL)
(See: SODOMY; HOMOSEXUALITY).

COITUS (ORAL)
(See: FELLATIO; CUNNILINGUS).

COITUS (PER OS)
(See: FELLATIO).

CONCUBINE
One of the women of a man with several wives, married with legal consent. It is not the same as adulteress.
(See: POLYGAMY).

COPULATION
Sexual act, generally human. But "animal copulation" can also be said; in this case, "intercourse" is preferred.
(See: COITUS).

CULT
"Ritual" and reverence dedicated to something tangible or supernatural.
(See: PHALLIC CULT).

CUNNILINGUS
Sexual practice which consists of licking the genital organs of the woman, and, in some cases, of her anus. There is also homosexual or lesbian cunnilingus. It corresponds to fellatio. It represents a form of oral coitus.

CHASTITY
Voluntary abstinence from genital activity before marriage. Demanded by Jewish-Christian civilization. It is not limited to them...
(See: CELIBACY).

DEFLOWERING
Generally, tearing the hymen under the pressure of the gland during the first sexual relationship. In this way, the woman "loses" her virginity. Deflowering can be ritual, by means of instruments.

DEPRAVATIONS
(See: SEXUAL DEVIATIONS).

EROTICISM
Concerning the excitement of the sexual instinct. According to M.A. Denegri, outside the limits of the idea of procreation...

EUNUCH
Male subject who lacks sexual organs due to castration or to congenital reasons.

EXHIBITIONISM
Exposition of the genitals in a generally exaggerated way, which differentiates "exhibitionism" from nakedness. Exhibitionist representations show the genitals alone, or in the context of a human figure.

FASTING
(See: ABSTINENCE).

FECUNDATION
The act of fecundation, or reproduction, done by coitus. Rites of (. . .) in which coitus is imitated or symbolized in order to increase the procreation of men, animals or plants.

FORNICATION
Sexual act between unmarried persons.

FELLATIO
Sexual practice consisting of licking the penis. Not always penis "suction" as done in fellatio. Self-fellatio is rare.
(See: CUNNILINGUS).

GYNECOCRACY
Government or social-politic preponderance of the female element. It is equivalent to matriarchy and the opposite of patriarchy.

GYNECOMAST
Development of female breasts in men.

HERMAPHRODITE
Subject endowed with two sexes. It is found on the Greco-Roman mythical plane and in other cultures, as well as in nature.

HETEROSEXUAL
Sexual relation between persons of different sexes.
(See: HOMOSEXUALITY).

HOMOPHILIA
(See: HOMOSEXUALITY).

HOMOSEXUALITY
Sexual relation between two men or two women. In popular terms, sexual relations between men. The passive homosexual acts as the woman and the active homosexual as the man. The word Homophilia extends the homosexual tendency to the sentimental sphere. The homosexual is not necessarily a hermaphrodite. Female homosexuality is commonly known as lesbianism.

INCEST
Marriage between intimate relations. Generally, for reasons of "blood purity" to perpetuate a dynasty.

LESBIANISM
(See: HOMOSEXUALITY).

LEVIRATE
The custom of inheriting the widow or widows of a brother.
(See: SORORATE).

LIBIDO
Word chosen by Freud (from the latin Libido = desire) to designate sexual energy. "Libidinous" is applied to the subject who is obsessed by sexual pleasure. For Jung, the "libido" has been desexed, and he considers it as general mental energy.

MAGIC-RELIGIOUS
Tendency to obtain supernatural favors by force (magic), or by religious goodness or supplication.

MANIPULATION
A caress is an amorous contact, sometimes "erotical", between two people of opposite sex. On the contrary, manipulation refers to touching the body, perhaps the sexual organs, the breasts, etc., with definite "erotical" intent.

MARRIAGE
Union accepted by the group, for purposes of sex and procreation. Nuptials generally represent the rite that begins the marriage.

MASOCHISM
Word derived from the Baron Sacher-Masoch (1836-1895). A sort of sexual stimulus in men or women felt through mental or physical pain.

MASTURBATION
Act by which, through genital manipulation, a high gradation of excitement is reached, which can lead to orgasm. It can be self masturbatory or not. The word "onanism" is equivalent to self-masturbation.

MATRIARCHY
(See: GYNECOCRACY)

MATRILOCAL
Marriage where the couple lives with the bride's family or group.
(See: PATRILOCAL).

MONOGAMY
Marriage to only one woman. The contrary of poligamy. It demands absolute faithfulness, adultery being punished.

NAKEDNESS
Appearing without clothes. In archaeological ages tattoos were used as a substitute for clothes. (Vicús, Peru). Nakedness can be of "erotical" nature or not.
(See: EXHIBITIONISM).

NUPTIALS
(See: MARRIAGE).

OBSCENE
Something "vulgar" applied frequently to the sexual sphere or to pornography. It can have "erotical" effects.

ONANISM
(See: MASTURBATION).

PAIDOPHILIA
Sensuous love by adults of either sex towards adolescents or children.
(See: PEDERASTY).

PATRIARCHY
Government by or preponderance of the male element.
(See: GYNECOCRACY).

PATRILOCAL
Marriage where a couple lives in the husband's community and is installed in his home.
(See: MATRILOCAL).

PEDERASTY
"Paidos" in Greek means "of the child". By extension, pederasts are subjects of either sex, sentitive in sexual ways to adolescents or children.
(See: PAIDOPHILIA).

PER ANUM
(See: SODOMY).

POLYANDRY
Marriage in which a woman can have more than one husband at a time. (Historically, the presence of Polyandry continues to be debated).
(See: POLYGAMY; POLYGINY).

PHALLUS
Erected penis, symbolizing sexual potency. From the Greek "Phallos".

POLYGAMY
(See: POLYGINY; MONOGAMY).

POLYGINY
Marriage in which a man can have more than one woman at a time. Also male polygamy. (See: CONCUBINE; POLYANDRY).

PORNOGRAPHY
(See: OBSCENE).

PROCREATION
(See: FECUNDATION).

PRONE
Position, in coitus, where the man (or the woman) is lying face down.

PROSTITUTION
Sexual trade. To offer oneself for payment or recompense. There is also male prostitution, of homosexual and heterosexual types.

SADISM
Word derived from the Marquis de Sade (born in 1740), applied to those who obtain sexual pleasure from having the other person suffer, etc. Masochism on the contrary is the pleasure of extreme suffering. Both expressions are often used in conjunction.

SATYR
Greco-roman mythological being with almost human face and breasts, but with goat's legs. Extremely sensuous. By extension, a man who suffers from sexual overexcitement, similar to nymphomania in women.

SODOMY
Anal coitus. In traditional terms, anti-natura or per anum sexual relation, homosexual and heterosexual. In a restricted sense, between persons of opposite sexes.

SORORATE
Practice of a younger girl marrying the widower of her deceased sister.
(See: LEVIRATE).

SUPINE
Position in coitus, in which the woman (or the man) is lying face upward.
(See: PRONE).

SEXUAL DEVIATIONS
Sexual acts considered as contrary to "normal". They can be of homosexual or heterosexual type: "sodomy", fellatio, paidophilia, etc.

SEXUAL THEME
Word coined by KD, which replaces that of "pornographic" art, by which term archaeological material with a sexual theme in Ancient Peru has been superficially classified.

SEXUAL VICES
(See: SEXUAL DEVIATIONS).

TABOO
Forbidden, within a magic context, so that when a taboo is broken it leads to disastrous occurences. Sexual taboos or prohibitions occur not only in Christianity. Incest, for instance, is taboo except for dynastic reasons.

TRAVESTITE
Person who wears clothes of the opposite sex.

VENEREAL DISEASES
Those whose origin is from sexual contact, as syphilis.

VENUS
Greco-roman female statue, archetype of beauty. By extention, female prehistoric statues with a (for today) grotesque look, due to their exaggerated obesity. (Willendorf). The "Mount of Venus" is the outer part of the body, in front of the vulva, covered by pubic hair.

VOTIVE
Sacred. There are sexual representations with votive or religious content.
(See: MAGIC-RELIGIOUS).

VULVA
Uro-genital external female organ, formed by the inner and outer folds, or labia, and the clitoris, as well as the Mount of Venus.

ZOOERASTY
Sexual intercourse with animals. From zoon: animal; and erastes: passionate lover. (Definition analyzed and divulged, in Peru, by M. A. Denegri).

INDEX

181